SPIRITUAL COMBAT

"And from the days of John the Baptist until now, the kingdom of heaven suffereth violence, and the violent bear it away."
—Matthew 11:12

THE
SPIRITUAL COMBAT

AND A TREATISE ON PEACE OF SOUL

by
Dom Lorenzo Scupoli
PRIEST OF THE CONGREGATION OF THE THEATINES

A Translation, revised by
William Lester, M.A.
and
Robert Mohan, M.A.

"Labor as a good soldier of Christ Jesus...For he also that striveth for the mastery, is not crowned, except he strive lawfully." —2 Timothy 2:3,5

TAN BOOKS AND PUBLISHERS, INC.
Rockford, Illinois 61105

Nihil Obstat: Edward A. Cerney, S.S.
                  Censor Deputatus

Imprimatur: ✠ Michael J. Curley, D.D.
                  Archbishop of Baltimore and Washington
                  June 16, 1945

Typesetting photographically reproduced by arrangement with Paulist Press, Mahwah, New Jersey.

Cover photo from *The Making of a Priest*, copyright © 1957 by Albert J. Nevins, M.M. Used with permission of Fr. Nevins.

Library of Congress Catalog Card No.: 90-70929

ISBN: 0-89555-405-4

Printed and bound in the United States of America.

TAN BOOKS AND PUBLISHERS, INC.
P.O. Box 424
Rockford, Illinois 61105

1990

"Therefore take unto you the armour of God, that you may be able to resist in the evil day, and to stand in all things perfect. Stand therefore, having your loins girt about with truth, and having on the breastplate of justice, and your feet shod with the preparation of the gospel of peace: In all things taking the shield of faith, wherewith you may be able to extinguish all the fiery darts of the most wicked one. And take unto you the helmet of salvation, and the sword of the Spirit (which is the word of God)." —*Ephesians 6:13-17*

THE *Spiritual Combat* is known as one of the greatest classics in ascetic theology. It has this in common with the *Following of Christ* that the identity of its author still lies in mystery.

Several seventeenth-century editions were published under the name of the Spanish Benedictine John of Castanzia. Some writers of the Society of Jesus have ascribed the book to the Jesuit Achilles Gagliardi. Most critics however consider the Italian Theatine Lawrence Scupoli as the author of this famous treatise. In his *Spiritualité Chrétienne*, Father P. Pourrat, S.S., ventures the opinion that the *Spiritual Combat* may well be the work of a religious order rather than that of an individual writer; for it was not originally composed such as we now have it. The first edition published in Venice in 1589 contained only twenty-four chapters; then, successive editions appeared with respectively thirty-three, thirty-seven, forty, and finally sixty-six chapters. It can also be said, in favor of this view, that there is an apparent lack of logical sequence between chapters in several parts of the work, and that the style of the latest edition differs considerably from that of the first.

Whatever may be the solution of this problem, doubt concerning the authorship of the *Spiritual Combat* can take nothing away from the value and utility of this "golden book," as St. Francis de Sales called it. It was "the favourite, the dear book" of this great master of the spiritual life who, for eighteen years, carried in his pocket a copy which he had received from Father Scupoli in Padua. The Saint read some pages of it every day, intrusted to its supernatural and human wisdom the guidance of his soul, and recommended it to all under his direction as being most attractive and most practical.

The purpose of the *Spiritual Combat* is clearly stated in the First Chapter; it is to lead the soul to the summit of spiritual perfection. What is meant by spiritual perfection? We are told that it does not consist in external works and practices, but is all interior; it means knowing and loving God, despising and mastering in us all our evil inclinations, that we may be able to submit and abandon ourselves entirely to God, out of love for Him.

Such is the goal at which we must aim. How can we reach it? By means of constant and courageous struggle against our evil nature, which tends to keep us away from that goal. This accounts for the title of the book, the *Spiritual Combat*, for it is truly "a course of spiritual strategy" * in which we learn how to conduct the fight against our evil tendencies, even the least of them, with the help of four essential weapons: 1—self-distrust; 2—confidence in God; 3—training in spiritual warfare through the proper use of our mental and physical powers; 4—prayer, both short or ejacula-

* Pourrat. Vol. 3, p. 360.

tory, and prolonged in the form of mental prayer. The detailed instructions given for a successful use of our faculties are especially characteristic of the *Spiritual Combat's* strategy.

The author's method is thorough, and, precisely because it goes deep into the roots of each subject, the reader would, at times, find it difficult to follow the trend of the thought, if the translation contained a certain number of involved sentences studded, here and there, with unfamiliar or abstract expressions.

The purpose of the present edition is to remove this difficulty. It is not a new translation from the Italian original; it is intended as a careful and thorough revision of the style and form of an already old English version. The revisers have broken up long paragraphs and sentences into shorter units, to relieve the attention of the reader. By simplifying or modifying the grammatical structure, when it was thought advisable, by substituting clearer or more familiar terms for obscure or archaic words, they have efficiently contributed in making accessible to all the treasures of spiritual doctrine and of wise spiritual direction contained in this remarkable and unique book.

B. F. MARCETTEAU, S.S.

Spiritual Director,
Theological College of the Catholic University
of America.

TABLE OF CONTENTS

THE
SPIRITUAL COMBAT

"For though we walk in the flesh, we do not war according to the flesh. For the weapons of our warfare are not carnal, but mighty to God unto the pulling down of fortifications, destroying counsels, and every height that exalteth itself against the knowledge of God, and bringing into captivity every understanding unto the obedience of Christ."
—2 Corinthians 10:3-5

CHAPTER ONE

Preliminary Words On Perfection.—In
What Does Christian Perfection Consist?
—We Must Fight in Order to Attain It.—
The Four Things Necessary for This
Combat

Christian Soul! If you seek to reach the loftiest
peak of perfection, and to unite yourself so intimately with God that you become one in spirit
with Him, you must first know the true nature
and perfection of spirituality in order to succeed
in the most sublime undertaking that can be expressed or imagined.

Some, who judge only by appearances, make it
consist in penances, in hair shirts, austerites of the
flesh, vigils, fasting, and similar bodily mortifications.

Others, particularly women, fancy themselves
extremely virtuous when they indulge in long
vocal prayers, hear several Masses, spend many
hours in church, and frequently receive Communion.

Others, and this does not exclude some of the
religious who have consecrated themselves to God,

1

think that perfection consists in perfect attendance in choir, in observing silence and retirement, and in a strict observance of their rule.

Consequently, different people place perfection in different practices. It is certain that they all equally deceive themselves.

Since exterior works are nothing more than dispositions for achieving true piety, or the effects of real piety, it cannot be said that Christian perfection and true piety consist in them.

They are, without doubt, powerful means for becoming truly perfect and truly holy. When used with discretion they are of unique value in supporting our nature which is always indifferent to good and inclined to evil; in repelling the attacks and escaping the snares of our common enemy; in obtaining from the Father of Mercies those helps that are so necessary for the faithful, and especially for beginners.

They are, moreover, precious fruits of the consummate virtue achieved in truly holy persons. Such men chastise their bodies either in punishment for past offences or for greater humiliation and subjection to their Creator. They seek solitude and observe silence that, withdrawn from the world, they may preserve themselves free from the least stain of sin, and speak only with heaven and its angels. Their time is spent in works of piety and in the service of God. They pray and meditate on the life and Passion of our Redeemer, not through curiosity, nor for the sake of some sensible pleasure arising from this, but from a desire of knowing better, on one hand, the grandeur of the Divine Goodness, and on the other hand, the depth of their own ingratitude. They do this in order to increase their love of God and detestation of self, to follow their Lord in shouldering His Cross, and in renouncing their own will. They receive the sacraments for no other reason than the honor of God, a closer union with Him and greater security from the power of the devil.

The situation is much different with those who ignorantly place their devotion in external acts, which frequently are the cause of their own downfall, and are of far deeper consequence than open crime. In themselves they are not evil, but only when wrongly applied. They are so attached to these acts that they utterly neglect to watch the inner movements of their hearts; but giving them free rein, they leave them a prey to their own corruption and to the tricks of the devil. It is then that this destroyer, seeing them go astray, not only encourages them to go on their way, but fills their imagination with empty ideas, making them believe that they already taste the joys of Paradise, the delights of Angels, that they see God face to face! As decoys, he does not hesitate to suggest in their meditation sublime, surprising, and ravishing thoughts, so that, forgetting the world and all earthly things, they are swept up to the third heaven.

A very little reflection on their conduct discloses their error and the great distance between them and that perfection of which we are now in search.

In every circumstance they love to be shown preference over others. They know no guide but their own private judgment, no rule but their own will. They are blind in their own affairs, ferret-eyed in regard to those of their neighbors, always ready to find fault.

Touch the empty reputation they think they possess, and of which they are extremely jealous. Order them to stop some of the devotions to which they are accustomed. Their amazement and vexation can hardly be expressed.

If God Himself, in order to open their eyes and to show them the true path of perfection, should send them crosses, sickness, or severe persecutions, the surest trials of His servant's fidelity, which never happen unless by His plan and permission, then the degenerate condition of their hearts is laid bare through their own extravagant pride. In all the events of this life, whether happy or not, they know nothing of a proper conformity to the will of God. They do not know how to yield to His almighty power, to submit to His judgments which are as just as they are secret and impenetrable. They do not know how to imitate Christ Crucified, as He humbled Himself before all men; nor do they know how to love their enemies as the instruments used by God's goodness to train them to self-denial and to help not only in their future salvation, but in a greater sanctification of their daily life.

This is the very reason why they are in imminent danger of being lost. With eyes blinded by self love, they examine themselves and their actions which are not otherwise blameworthy, and they are inflated with vanity. They conclude that they are far advanced towards God and they readily look down on their neighbor: in fact, their pride often will so increase their blindness, that their conversion cannot be effected without a miracle of grace.

Experience proves that acknowledged sinners are reformed with less difficulty than those who wilfully hide themselves under the cloak of a false virtue.

From this you can easily understand that the spiritual life does not consist in the practices enumerated above, if they are considered only in their outward appearance.

It actually consists in knowing the infinite greatness and goodness of God, together with a true sense of our own weakness and tendency to evil, in loving God and hating ourselves, in humbling ourselves not only before Him, but, for His sake, before all men, in renouncing entirely our own will in order to follow His. It consists, finally, in doing all of this solely for the glory of His holy name, for only one purpose—to please Him, for only one motive—that He should be loved and served by all His creatures.

These are the dictates of that law of love which the Holy Ghost has written on the hearts of the faithful. This is the way we must practice that self-denial so earnestly recommended by our

Saviour in the Gospel. This it is that renders His yoke so sweet, His burden so light. In short, the perfect obedience that our divine Master has enjoined by word and example consists in this.

Since, therefore, you seek the highest degree of perfection, you must wage continual warfare against yourself and employ your entire strength in demolishing each vicious inclination, however trivial. Consequently, in preparing for the combat you must summon up all your resolution and courage. No one shall be rewarded with a crown who has not fought courageously.

But remember that as no war can be carried on with greater fierceness, the forces, no other than ourselves, being equal on both sides, so the victory when gained is most pleasing to God and most glorious to the conqueror.

For whoever has the courage to conquer his passions, to subdue his appetites, and repulse even the least motions of his own will, performs an action more meritorious in the sight of God than if, without this, he should tear his flesh with the sharpest disciplines, fast with greater austerity than the ancient Fathers of the Desert, or convert multitudes of sinners.

It is true, considering things in themselves, that the conversion of a soul is, without doubt, infinitely more acceptable to the divine Majesty than the mortification of a disorderly affection. Yet every person, in his own particular sphere, should begin with what is immediately required of him.

Now what God expects of us, above all else, is

a serious application to conquering our passions; and this is more properly the accomplishment of our duty than if, with uncontrolled appetite, we should do Him a greater service.

Now that you know what Christian perfection is and that, in order to attain it, you must resolve on a perpetual war with yourself, begin by providing yourself with four weapons without which it is impossible to gain the victory in this spiritual combat. These four things are: distrust of one's self, confidence in God, proper use of the faculties of body and mind, and the duty of prayer.

With the help of God's grace, these will be treated clearly and concisely in the following chapters.

CHAPTER TWO

Concerning Distrust of Self

Distrust of self is so absolutely requisite in the spiritual combat that without this virtue we cannot expect to defeat our weakest passions, much less gain a complete victory. This important truth should be deeply embedded in our hearts; for, although in ourselves we are nothing, we are too apt to overestimate our own abilties and to conclude falsely that we are of some importance. This vice springs from the corruption of our nature. But the more natural a thing is, the more difficult it is to be discovered.

But God, to Whom nothing is secret, looks upon this with horror, because it is His will that we should be convinced we possess only that virtue and grace which comes from Him alone, and that without Him we are incapable of one meritorious thought.

This distrust of our own strength is a gift from Heaven, bestowed by God on those He loves. It is granted sometimes through His holy inspiration, sometimes through severe afflictions, or almost insurmountable temptations and other ways which are unknown to us. Yet He expects that we will do everything within our power to obtain it. And we certainly will obtain it if, with the grace of God, we seriously employ the following four means.

First. We must meditate upon our own weakness. Consider that fact that, being nothing in ourselves, we cannot, without divine assistance, accomplish the smallest good or advance the smallest step towards heaven.

Second. We must beg of God, with great humility and fervor, this eminent virtue which must come from Him alone. Let us begin by acknowledging not only that we do not possess it, but that of ourselves we are utterly incapable of acquiring it. Then let us cast ourselves at the feet of our Lord and earnestly beg Him to grant our request. We must do this with firm confidence that we will be heard if we patiently await the effect of our prayer, and persevere in it as long as it pleases divine Providence.

Third. We must gradually accustom ourselves to distrust our own strength, to dread the illusions of our own mind, the strong tendency of our nature to sin, and the overwhelming number of enemies that surround us. Their subtlety, experience, and strength surpass ours, for they can transform themselves into angels of light and lie in ambush for us as we advance towards heaven.

Fourth. As often as we commit a fault, we must examine ourselves in order to discover our vulnerable points. God permits us to fall only that we may gain a deeper insight into ourselves, that we may learn to despise ourselves as wretched creatures and to desire honestly to be disregarded by others. Without this we cannot hope to obtain a distrust of self which is rooted in humility and the knowledge of our own weakness.

Whoever seeks to approach the eternal truth and fountain of all light must know himself thoroughly. He must not imitate the pride of those who obtain no other knowledge than what their sins provide, and who begin to open their eyes only when they are plunged into some disgraceful and unforeseen debacle. This happens through God's permission that they may know their own weakness, and, by sad experience, learn not to rely on their own strength. God seldom applies so severe a remedy against their presumption unless more proper means have failed.

Briefly, He permits persons to sin more or less grievously in proportion to their pride, and, if there were any as free from pride as the Blessed Virgin, I dare say they would never fall. As often as you commit a fault, therefore, immediately strive to probe your inner consciousness; earnestly beg our Lord to enlighten you, that you may see yourself as you are in His sight, and presume no more on your strength. Otherwise you will fall again into the same faults, or perhaps much greater ones to the eternal ruin of your soul.

CHAPTER THREE

CONFIDENCE IN GOD

ALTHOUGH DISTRUST of self is absolutely necessary in the spiritual combat, nevertheless, if this is all we have to rely on, we will soon be routed, plundered, and subdued by the enemy. To it, therefore, we must join firm confidence in God, the Author of all good, from Whom alone the victory must be expected. Since it is certain that, in ourselves, we are nothing, and that dangerous misfortunes continually threaten us, reason itself suggests distrust of our own strength. But if we are fully convinced of our weakness, we shall gain, through the assistance of God, very great victories over our enemies. There is nothing of greater efficacy in obtaining the assistance of heaven than placing complete confidence in God. We have four means of acquiring this excellent virtue.

First. To ask it with great humility.

Second. To contemplate with an ardent faith the immense power and infinite wisdom of the Supreme Being. To Him nothing is difficult; His goodness is unlimited; His love for those who serve Him is always ready to supply them with the necessities for their spiritual life, and for gaining a complete victory over themselves.

All that He demands is that they turn to Him with complete confidence. Can anything be more reasonable? The amiable Shepherd for thirty-three years or more sought after the lost sheep through thorn-roughened ways, with so much pain that it cost Him the last drop of His sacred blood. When this devoted Shepherd sees His strayed sheep finally returning to Him with the desire of being guided in the future by Him alone, and with a sincere, though perhaps weak intention of obeying Him, is it possible that He would not look upon it with pity, listen to its cries, and bear it upon His shoulders to the fold? Doubtless He is greatly pleased to see it united again to the flock, and invites the Angels to rejoice with Him on the occasion.

For if He searches so diligently after the drachma in the Gospel, which is a figure of the sinner, if He leaves nothing untouched in order to find it, can He reject those who, like sheep longing to see their Shepherd, return to the fold? Can it be imagined that the Spouse of our souls, Who diligently seeks to take possession of our hearts, Whose greatest delight is to communicate Himself to us and heap continual blessings on us— can it be imagined that He, finding the door open, and hearing us beg to be honored by His presence, will do anything but grant our request?

Third. Another means of acquiring this salutary confidence is frequently to recall what we are assured of in the Holy Scriptures, the witnesses of truth, in a thousand different places—that no one who puts his trust in God will be defeated.

Fourth. The final means of acquiring both distrust of self and confidence in God is that before attempting to perform any good action, or to encounter some failing, we should look at our own weakness on the one hand, and on the other contemplate the infinite power, wisdom, and goodness of God. Balancing what we fear from ourselves with what we hope from God, we shall courageously undergo the greatest difficulties and severest trials. Joining these weapons to prayer, as we shall see later, we shall be able to execute the greatest plans and gain decisive victories.

But if we neglect this method, though we may flatter ourselves that we are actuated by a principle of confidence in God, we will usually be deceived. Presumption is so natural to man that, without notice, it insinuates itself into the confidence he imagines he has in God and the distrust he fancies he has of himself.

Consequently, in order to destroy all presumption and to sanctify every action with the two virtues opposite to this vice, the consideration of one's own weakness must precede that of the divine Power. Both of these must precede all undertakings.

CHAPTER FOUR

How to Discover Whether We Distrust Ourselves and Place Our Confidence in God

THE PRESUMPTUOUS MAN is convinced that he has acquired a distrust of himself and confidence in God, but his mistake is never more apparent than when some fault is committed. For, if he yields to anger and despairs of advancing in the way of virtue, it is evident that he placed his confidence in himself and not in God. The greater the anxiety and despondence, the greater is the certainty of his guilt.

The man who has a deep distrust of himself and places great confidence in God is not at all surprised if he commits a fault. He does not abandon himself to confused despair; he correctly attributes what has happened to his own weakness and lack of confidence in God. Thus he learns to distrust himself more, and he places all his hopes in the assistance of the Almighty. He detests beyond all things the sin into which he has fallen; he condemns the passion or criminal habit that occasioned his fall; he conceives a deep sorrow for his offence against God. But his sorrow, accompanied by peace of mind, does not interrupt the method he has laid down, nor does it prevent the pursuit of his enemies to their final destruction.

I sincerely wish that what has been proposed here would be attentively considered by many who think they are very devout. Yet from the moment they commit a fault they will not be pacified, but hurry away to their director, more to rid themselves of the distress arising from self-love than from any other motive. Their principal care should be to wash away the guilt of sin in the sacrament of Penance and to fortify themselves with the Eucharist against a relapse.

CHAPTER FIVE

THE MISTAKE OF CONSIDERING COWARDICE A VIRTUE

MANY ARE ALSO deceived in this way. They ascribe to virtue the cowardice and anxiety that arises from sin. Although this weakness is accompanied by some sorrow, it is founded on a hidden pride and presumption of one's own strength. Thus the man who thinks he is far advanced in virtue looks with too much indifference on temptations, and finds by sad experience that, like other men, he is subject to weakness. He is astonished at his fall, and finding himself deceived in his expectations, sinks into sorrow and despair.

This never happens to the humble man who does not presume on his own strength, but places his trust in God alone. If he commits a fault, it occasions no surprise or anxiety, because he discovers by that light of truth which is his guide that his fall is due to his natural instability and weakness.

CHAPTER SIX

FURTHER ADVICE ON HOW TO OBTAIN A DISTRUST OF ONESELF AND CONFIDENCE IN GOD

As ALL OUR STRENGTH for conquering the enemy derives from distrust of self and confidence in God, I think I should give some additional advice, very necessary for obtaining these virtues.

In the first place, everyone must be convinced that neither all natural or acquired abilities, nor all supernatural gifts or perfect knowledge of the Scriptures, nor even whole ages spent in the service of his Creator, can enable him to do the will of God. He cannot perform his duty unless the Hand of the Almighty sustains him as often as any good action is to be done, temptation to be overcome, dangers to be avoided, or crosses to be borne according to the will of God. This truth must be kept in mind every day, hour, and moment of his life. In this way he will lose all presumption and will never rashly trust in himself.

In order to acquire complete confidence in God, he must firmly believe that He is as perfectly capable of conquering a great number of enemies as a few, the strong and experienced as the weak and inexperienced. Consequently, although a soul is overwhelmed by sins, although it has labored in vain to tear away from vice and follow virtue, although it should find its inclination to

17

evil increasing daily instead of diminishing in favor of virtue, yet it must not fail to place its confidence in God; it must not be discouraged or abandon its spiritual works. On the contrary, it must arouse itself to new fervor and redouble its efforts against the enemy.

In this kind of battle, the victory will be won by him who has the courage not to throw down his arms or put aside his confidence in God. His assistance is always present for those that fight His battles, though He may sometimes permit them to be wounded. Persevere to the end. Victory depends on this. There is a swift and effective remedy for the wounds of anyone who fights for God's cause and who places his entire trust in Him. When he least expects it, he will see his enemy at his feet.

CHAPTER SEVEN

The Right Use of Our Faculties. The Understanding Must First be Free of Ignorance and Curiosity

IF WE ENGAGE in the spiritual combat with no other weapons than a distrust of self and confidence in God, we will not only be deprived of a victory over our passions, but we must expect frequently to commit greater blunders. It is necessary, therefore, to employ correctly the faculties of body and soul, the third means we proposed as requisite for the attainment of perfection.

Let us begin with regulating the understanding and the will. The understanding must be freed from two great defects under which it frequently labors. The first is ignorance. This prevents the attainment of truth, the proper object of its inquiries. Exercise makes it lucid and brightens it, so that it can clearly discern how to purge the soul of all irregular attachments and adorn it with the necessary virtues. The means of accomplishing this are as follows.

The primary means is prayer, by which is sought the light of the Holy Spirit, Who never rejects those who earnestly seek God, who delight in obeying His law, and who, in all decisons, submit their own judgment to that of their superiors.

The second is a persistent application to the

serious and diligent examination of every object in order to distinguish the good from the evil. A judgment is formed which is not in accord with external appearances, the testimony of our senses, or the standards of a corrupt world, but which is conformable to the judgment of the Holy Spirit.

Then we shall clearly see that what the world pursues with such eagerness and affection is mere vanity and illusion; that ambition and pleasure are dreams which, once shattered, are succeeded by sorrow and regret; that ignominy is a subject of glory, and sufferings a source of joy; that nothing can be more noble or approach the divine nature more closely than to forgive those who injure us, and to return good for evil.

We shall see clearly that it is greater to despise the world than to have it at one's command; that it is infinitely preferable to submit to the humblest of men for God's sake, than to command kings and princes; that an humble knowledge of ourselves surpasses the deepest sciences; in short, that greater praise is due to him who curbs his passions on the most trivial occasions, than to him who conquers the strongest cities, defeats entire armies, or even works miracles and raises the dead to life.

CHAPTER EIGHT

AN OBSTACLE TO FORMING A CORRECT JUDGMENT. AN AID TO THE FORMATION OF A CORRECT JUDGMENT

ANY DIFFICULTY in forming a correct judgment of the things we have just mentioned, and of many others also, arises from a superficial notion of love and hatred, from a hasty conception we might form of them at first glance. Since our reason is influenced by blind passions, everything appears in a far different light from that in which it should be considered. Whoever, therefore, desires to entrench himself against such a dangerous and common illusion must carefully preserve his heart free from all inordinate affection.

When an object presents itself, let the understanding weigh its merits with mature deliberation before the will is permitted to embrace it if agreeable, or reject it if otherwise.

As long as the understanding remains unbiased by the passions, it will easily distinguish between truth and falsehoood, between real evil masquerading as good, and real good under the false appearance of evil. However, as soon as the will is moved either to love or hatred by the object, the understanding cannot form a true estimate of it, because the affection disguises it and imprints an incorrect idea. When this is again presented to the will which already is prepossessed, it redoubles its love or hatred, pushes beyond all limits, and is utterly deaf to the voice of reason.

In this distorted confusion, the understanding plunges deeper and deeper into error and represents the object to the will in vivid colors of good and evil.

Consequently, whenever the rule laid down before, which is of the greatest importance on this occasion, is neglected, the two noblest faculties of the soul are bewildered in a network of error, darkness and confusion. Happy are those who strip themselves of all attachment to creatures and then endeavor to discover the true nature of things before they permit their affections to be attached, who formulate their judgments by the principles of reason, and particularly by the supernatural guides which the Holy Spirit willingly communicates, either immediately from Himself, or through those whom He has appointed as our directors.

But remember; this advice very frequently must be followed more precisely in those things which are good in themselves, than in those which are not completely good, because there is greater danger of deception. They usually engender a misconceived enthusiasm. Do nothing rashly, therefore, since a single unobserved factor of time or place may ruin everything. A great fault may be committed in the way a thing is done, as is true of many who have fashioned their own destruction in the practice of the holiest exercises.

CHAPTER NINE

ANOTHER METHOD TO PREVENT DECEPTION OF THE UNDERSTANDING

CURIOSITY IS ANOTHER vice from which the mind must be free. If we indulge in vain, frivolous, or sinful dreams, our minds will become incapable of choosing the proper mortification of our disorderly affections.

All earthly things, except those absolutely necessary, must die through our complete disregard for them, even though they are not wrong in themselves. We must control our minds and not permit them to wander aimlessly about. Our minds must become insensible to mundane projects, to gossip, to the feverish search for news. Our indifference to the affairs of this world must give them a dream-like quality.

The same holds true for heavenly things. We must be discreet and humble. Our greatest ambition must be to see the crucified Christ always before us, His life and death, what efforts He demands of us.

Seek nothing beyond this. It will please the divine Master. His real friends ask only for those things that will enable them to fulfill His commissions. Any other desire, any other quest, is but self-love, spiritual pride, an encirclement by the devil.

Such a disciplined conduct is well fortified against the assaults of the devil. When this skilled opponent sees the fervor of persons beginning spiritual exercises and the fixed resolution of their wills, he insinuates his subtleties into their understanding. A break-through here permits him to push his way to the will. He is then the master of both these faculties.

As a feint, he inflates their imagination in moments of prayer, suggesting elevated sentiments. He works particularly on those who are curious and discerning by nature, who are subject to self-conceit and are fond of their own schemes. His aim, of course, is to amuse them with idle dreams and the sensible pleasure they afford so that, drugged with a false sense of appreciation of God, they may forget to cleanse their hearts, to examine themselves, and to practice mortification. In this way they become inflated with pride, and they idolize their own understanding.

Having become accustomed to consult no one but themselves, they finally are persuaded that they no longer need the advice or assistance of others.

It is a deadly, an almost incurable disease. It is much more difficult to remedy pride of the understanding than that of the heart. As soon as pride of the heart is discovered by the intelligence, it can be removed by a voluntary submission to proper authorities. But if a persons imagines, and persists in maintaining, that he is wiser than his superiors, how will his deception be shattered?

How will he discover his error? To whose judgment will he submit so long as he considers himself wiser than the rest of the world?

If the understanding, the searchlight of the soul, which alone can discover and rectify the vanity of the heart, is itself blinded and swollen with pride, who is able to cure it?

If the light changes to darkness, if the leader is treacherous, what will happen to the rest?

Be on guard, therefore, against such a fatal attack. Never let it overwhelm your minds.

We must train ourselves to conform to the judgment of others. Without carrying our notions of spirituality too high, let us become enamoured with the folly and simplicity recommended so highly by the Apostle; then shall we surpass Solomon himself in wisdom.

CHAPTER TEN

THE EXERCISE OF THE WILL. THE END TO WHICH ALL OF OUR ACTIONS, INTERIOR AND EXTERIOR, SHOULD BE DIRECTED

WE HAVE SPOKEN concerning the necessity of regulating one's understanding. It is necessary also to control one's will so that it is not abandoned to its own inclinations, but it is conformed entirely to the will of God.

It must be observed that it is not sufficient to desire, or even to execute what is most pleasing to God. It is also requisite to desire and to perform our action under the influence of His grace, and out of a willingness to please Him.

Here will arise the greatest struggle with our nature, constantly thirsty for its own pleasure. Even in lofty spiritual undertakings, it seeks its own satisfaction, residing there without the least scruple, since there is no apparent evil. The following is the result. We begin acts of religion not from the sole motive of doing the will of God, but for a sensible pleasure that often accompanies such acts.

The illusion is still more subtle as the object of our affection is more commendable in itself. Who would imagine that self-love, criminal as it is, should prompt us to unite ourselves to God? That in our desire to possess Him we should pursue

our own interests rather than His glory and the
accomplishment of His will, which should be the
only motive for those who love Him, seek Him,
and profess to keep His laws?

If we desire to avoid such a dangerous obstacle,
we must accustom ourselves not to desire or execute anything unless it is through the impulse of
the Holy Spirit, combined with a pure intention
of honoring Him Who desires to be not only the
first Principle, but also the last End of our every
word and action, through the observance of the
following method.

As soon as an opportunity presents itself to perform such a good action, we must prevent our
heart from seizing on it before we have considered
God. This will enable us to know whether it co-
incides with His will, and whether we desire it
solely because it is pleasing to Him.

When our will is controlled and directed in
this way by the will of God, it is motivated only
with the desire to conform entirely to Him, and
to further His glory. The same method is to be
followed in rejecting whatever is contrary to His
will. The first move is to raise our minds to God
to know what is displeasing to Him, and then be
satisfied that in its rejection we conform to His
holy will.

We must remember that it is extremely difficult
to discover the deceptions of our fallen nature. It
is always fond of making itself, for very question-
able motives, the focal point of all things; it flat-
ters by persuading us that in all our actions our

only motive is to please God. What we accept or reject, then, is actually done to please ourselves, while we erroneously imagine that we act out of a desire to please, or a dread of displeasing, our Sovereign Lord.

The most effective remedy against evil is purity of heart. Everyone engaged in the spiritual combat must be armed with it, discarding the old man and putting on the new. The remedy is applied in this way. In everything that we undertake, pursue, or reject, we divest ourselves of all human considerations, and do only what is conformable to the will of God.

It may happen that in many things we do, and especially in the interior impulses of the heart, or in swiftly transient exterior actions, we may not always be conscious of the influence of this motive. But at least we should be so disposed that virtually and habitually we act from the viewpoint of pleasing God.

In more prolonged activities this virtual intention is not sufficient. It should be frequently renewed and developed to its full stature in purity and fervor. Without this, we run the great risk of deception by self-love, which always prefers the creature to the Creator and so deceives that, in a short time, we are imperceptibly drawn from our primary intention.

Well meaning but vulnerable persons generally set out with no other purpose than to please God. But by degrees they permit themselves, without knowing it, to be lured away by vanity. They forget the divine will which first influenced them and are completely absorbed in the satisfaction afforded by their actions, and in the advantages and rewards they expect. If it happens that, while they think they are accomplishing great things, Providence permits them to be interrupted by sickness or some accident, they are immediately dissatisfied, criticizing everyone about them, and sometimes even God Himself. This is clear evidence that the motive, the force behind their actions was bad.

Anyone who acts under the influence of divine grace and only to please God is indifferent as to his course of action. Or, if he is inclined to some particular activity, he completely submits to Providence the manner and time of doing it. He is perfectly resigned to whatever success attends his undertakings, and his heart desires nothing but the accomplishment of the divine will.

Therefore, let everyone examine himself, let him direct all his actions to this most excellent and noble end. If he discovers that he is performing a work of piety in order to avoid punishment, or to gain the rewards of the future life, he should establish as the end of his undertaking the will of God, Who requires that we avoid hell and gain heaven.

It is not within man's power to realize the efficacy of this motive. The least action, no matter how insignificant, performed for His sake, greatly surpasses actions which, although of greater significance, are done for other motives.

For example, a small alms, given solely in honor of God, is infinitely more agreeable to Him than if, from some other motive, large possessions are abandoned, even if this is done from a desire to gain the kingdom of heaven. And this, in itself, is a highly commendable motive, and worthy of our consideration.

The practice of performing all of our actions solely from the intention of pleasing God may be difficult at first. With the passing of time it will become familiar and even delightful, if we strive to find God in all sincerity of heart, if we continually long for Him, the only and greatest Good, deserving to be sought, valued, and loved by all His creatures. The more attentively we contemplate the greatness and goodness of God, the more frequently and tenderly our affections will turn to that divine Object. In this way we will more quickly, and with greater facility, obtain the habit of directing all our actions to His glory.

In conclusion, there is a final way of acting in complete accordance with this very excellent and elevated motive. This is fervently to petition our Lord for grace and frequently to consider the infinite benefits He has already given us, and which He continues to bestow every moment from an undeserved and disinterested affection.

CHAPTER ELEVEN

SOME CONSIDERATIONS WHICH WILL INCLINE THE WILL TO SEEK ONLY WHAT IS PLEASING TO GOD

IN ORDER TO INCLINE our will to fulfill exactly the will of God and to promote His glory, let us remember that He has set the example by loving and honoring us in a thousand different ways. He created us out of nothing, after His own likeness, and He subordinated all other things to our use.

In our redemption He passed by the most brilliant angel to choose His only Son, Who paid the price of the world, not with perishable gold or silver, but with His sacred blood in a death as cruel as it was wretched.

He continually guards us from the fury of our enemies, He fights for us with His grace, and, to nourish and strengthen us, He is always ready to feed us with the precious body of His Son in the sacrament of the Altar. Do not these constitute convincing proofs of God's tremendous love for us? Who can understand the immensity of His love for such wretched creatures? What should be our gratitude towards so generous a benefactor!

If the great men of the world think they are obliged to do something in return for the respect paid them, even by those inferior as to position and wealth, what return ought not the very worms of the earth make when honored with such remarkable love and esteem by the sovereign Lord of the Universe?

In particular, we must never forget that His majesty is infinitely worthy of our service, a service motivated by a single principle of love, whose only object is His will and desire.

CHAPTER TWELVE

The Opposition Within Man's Twofold Nature

Man has a twofold nature, the one superior, the other inferior. The first is generally termed reason, the second is called appetite, sensuality, or passion. Reason is the distinguishing property of man, and he is not considered responsible for the primary impulses of his appetite unless his superior faculty confirms the choice.

The entire spiritual warfare, consequently, consists in this: the rational faculty is placed between the divine will above it and the sensitive appetite below it, and is attacked from both sides—God moving it by His grace, and the flesh by its appetites strive for victory.

It is apparent, then, that inconceivable difficulties arise when persons who during their youth have contracted vicious habits resolve to change their life, mortify their passions, and break with the world in order to devote themselves to the service of God.

The will is violently attacked by divine grace and by its own sensual appetites, and wherever it turns, it absorbs these withering attacks with the greatest difficulty.

This onslaught is not experienced by those who are firmly settled in their way of life, whether in virtue by conforming to the will of God, or in vice by indulging their sensual desires.

No one should delude himself that he can acquire virtue and serve God in the proper way, unless he is willing to undergo a violent struggle. He must conquer the difficulty he will experience when he deprives himself of the pleasures, great or small, to which he has been viciously attached.

The result is that very few attain any great degree of perfection. After conquering their greatest vice, after undergoing tremendous exertions, they lose courage and fail to pursue their objective. And this when only small trials are to be overcome, such as subduing the feeble remnants of their own will, and annihilating some weaker passions which revive and then completely regain their hearts.

Many persons of this type, for example, do not take what belongs to others, but they are passionately attached to what is their own. They do not use any illegal methods of aggrandizement, but instead of spurning advancement, they are fond of it and seek it by any means they think lawful. They observe the appointed fasts, but, on other days, they indulge in the most exotic delicacies. They are very careful to observe chastity, and yet they refuse to give up their favorite amusements, even though they constitute great obstacles to a spiritual life and real union with God. Since these things are so highly dangerous, particularly for those who do not recognize their bad results, they must be dealt with very cautiously.

Without such caution, we may be assured that

most of our good acts will have as attendants, slothfulness, vanity, human respect, hidden imperfections, conceit, and a desire for the notice and approval of others.

Anyone who neglects this particular aspect of the problem not only makes no progress on the road to salvation, but even loses ground and is in danger of falling back into his former vicious practices. He does not aim at solid virtue and is unconscious of the great favor God has done him by freeing him from the despotism of the devil. He is ignorant of the danger that surrounds him, and is enchanted by a false and deceptive peace.

It is necessary here to point out an illusion which must be feared, as it is not easily discovered. Many who begin a spiritual life have too great a love for themselves (if they can be said to truly love themselves), and they single out certain exercises that are most pleasant. But they avoid anything that is disagreeable to their inclinations, or equipped to mortify their passions, against which their entire force should be thrown in this spiritual struggle.

Every means must be exploited to make them enjoy the hazards they encountered in conquering their inclinations. On this everything depends. The greater the resolution shown in surmounting the first obstacles that occur, the swifter and more brilliantly will victory accompany them. With courage, therefore, let them expect nothing but hardship in this warfare and wait patiently for victory and its rewards. Then they may be confident that they will not be disappointed.

CHAPTER THIRTEEN

How We Are to Encounter Sensuality. What the Will Must Do to Acquire Virtuous Habits

WHEN OUR CREATOR and sensuality struggle for possession of our hearts, victory will follow the side of Heaven, if we use the following tactics.

1. The first impulses of the sensual appetite that oppose reason must be carefully checked, that the will should not give its consent to them.

2. After this is done, they may be released in order to give them a greater setback.

3. A third trial may be given in order to steel ourselves to repulse them with generous contempt. It is necessary to observe that these methods of arousing the passions are not to be used where chastity is involved. We shall speak of this later.

4. Lastly, it is extremely important to perform acts of those virtues which are opposed to the vicious inclinations we encounter. The following example will place this in a clear light.

You are, it may be supposed, subject to impatience. Recollect yourself—examine what is passing through your mind. You will observe that the trouble which first arose in the lower appetite attempts to control the will and the higher faculties.

Here, as I mentioned previously, you must stop

it, and prevent it from prevailing on the will. Do not leave the field until your enemy is entirely subdued, and reduced in proper subjection to the reason.

But you see the cleverness of the tempter! If he finds out that you courageously overcome impetuous passion, he not only ceases to light it in your heart, but even assists in banking the fire for the present. His plan is to prevent the attainment of the contrary virtue by a steady resistance, and to inflate you with the vanity of thinking you are a great soldier for having defeated your enemy in such a short time.

You must renew this procedure. Bring to mind what first moved you to impatience. When you recognize the same emotion rising in your lower appetite, mobilize the entire force of your will to suppress it.

It frequently happens that after the most strenuous engagements with the enemy, which have been motivated by the desire of fulfilling our duty and pleasing God, we are not entirely out of the danger of defeat by a third attack. We must once more fight the passion we combated, and arouse not only hatred, but also contempt and horror of it.

Briefly, if you want to equip your soul with virtue and acquire habitual sanctity, it is necessary to practice frequent acts of the virtue which is contrary to your vicious inclinations.

For example, if you want to acquire a high degree of patience, you must not consider it sufficient to employ the three types of weapon that have been mentioned in order to overcome all the impatience occasioned by the contempt you endure from others. You must proceed even to an affection for the contempt itself; to wish for its repetition, even from the same persons; to resolve to endure patiently even greater insults.

The reason we must form acts which are directly contrary to our failings, if we desire to attain perfection, is this—other acts of virtue, however efficacious and frequent, do not strike directly at the root of the evil.

To continue the example—although you do not give consent to impulses of anger, but deal with them in the ways described, yet be certain of this. Unless you accustom yourself to enjoy contempt and be happy in it, you will never entirely root out the vice of impatience, for it springs up from a dread of contempt and a fondness for the applause of men.

As long as the root of this weed is not torn out, it will sprout again, and your virtue will perish. In time, you may discover that you are stripped of good habits and in continual danger of falling back into your former disorders. Never hope to acquire solid virtue unless you destroy your own particular failings by performing frequent acts which are directly opposed to them.

I say frequent acts—for frequent acts are necessary to build a virtuous habit, just as many sins are required to confirm oneself in a vicious habit. In fact, a greater number of acts must be performed in the former instance, because our weakened nature resists the one side as much as it assists the other.

You will observe that certain virtues cannot be acquired without performing external acts corresponding to the interior dispositions. This is true with regard to patience. You must not only speak with great charity and mildness to those who have injured you, no matter how great the offence, but even help them to the limit of your abilities.

Although these acts, whether external or internal, may seem insignificant, and even greatly repugnant, do not omit them. However small they may seem, they will certainly support you in the struggle and will greatly contribute to your victory.

Guard your mind, therefore, and do not be content to restrain the most violent surges of passion; resist the most minute. They generally lead to the greater and pave the way to deeply vicious habits.

Does not experience teach us that many who neglect to mortify their passions in trivialities, although they show courage in heroic trials, are unexpectedly trapped, and viciously attacked by enemies that had never been entirely destroyed?

There is another thing most sincerely recommended. Mortify your inclinations, even when the object in itself is lawful, but not necessary. It will facilitate victory on other occasions; you will gain experience and strength against temptation, and present yourself as acceptable to your Saviour.

This is sincere advice. Do not fail to exert yourself in the practices mentioned. They are absolutely requisite for the perfect formation of your soul. You will quickly gain a great victory over yourself. You will advance rapidly on the path of virtue. Your life will become spiritual, not only in appearance, but in reality.

If you follow other methods, however excellent you consider them, though you taste the greatest spiritual delights, though you imagine yourself intimately united to God, you can depend on this; you will never acquire solid virtue, nor know what true spirituality is. This does not, as has been shown in the first chapter, consist in acts that are agreeable or pleasant to our nature, but in those that crucify it and all its irregular attractions.

In this way, man, renewed by his acquired virtues, unites himself completely to his Creator and crucified Saviour. It is certain that vicious habits are contracted by several acts of the will which yield to sensual appetites. In the same way, Evangelical perfection is attained by repeated acts of the will conforming itself to the will of God, Who moves it to practice different virtues at different times.

The will incurs no guilt unless it gives consent to an act, even if the entire force of the lower appetite is exerted towards a guilty end. On the other hand, the will cannot be sanctified and united to God, however strong the grace attracting it, unless it co-operates with that grace by interior acts, and, if requisite, by exterior acts.

CHAPTER FOURTEEN

What to Do When the Will is Apparently Overpowered, and Unable to Resist the Sensual Appetites

IF YOU EVER FEAR that your will should fall before the lower appetite, or other enemies that attempt to overcome it; if you perceive that your courage and determination are failing, hold your ground— do not retreat from the field. You must regard the victory as your own as long as you are not completely overcome.

Just as your will does not need the consent of the lower appetite to make its choice, in the same way the liberty of the will remains intact despite any violence that this interior enemy may use. An absolute dominion has been given us by the Almighty. All the senses, the evil spirits, and the whole created universe banded together cannot diminish the liberty of the will in acting as often, in any manner, and to any end that it desires.

But, if at times temptations press you so hard that your will, almost overpowered, seems to lack sufficient strength to resist any longer, do not be disheartened, or throw down your arms. Defend yourself and cry out: "I shall never surrender to you! I shall not submit to you!" Act like a person who, struggling with a stubborn enemy and being unable to pierce him with the point, attacks him with the hilt of the sword. Watch how he tries to break free, to retreat in order to charge with greater strength, and to kill the enemy with one fatal blow!

This teaches you to withdraw frequently into yourself. Recall your insignificance, your inability to accomplish anything. You will then place great confidence in the almighty power of God, so that you will be able, through His grace, to attack and conquer the passions that oppose you. Here you must implore: "My Lord, My God! Jesus! Mary! Do not abandon your soldier! Do not permit me to be conquered by this temptation!"

Whenever the enemy gives you a breathing spell, call up your understanding to reinforce your will. Strengthen it with motives that will raise its courage and give it new life for the fight.

For example, if you are unjustly accused or harmed in some other way, and, in desperation, are tempted to lose all patience, try to check yourself by reflecting on these points:

1. Consider whether you might not deserve the unpleasantness you are undergoing, and whether you have not brought it upon yourself. If you are in any way to blame, it is proper that you patiently endure the agony of the wound which you yourself have occasioned.

2. However, if you are not guilty on this score, glance back at some past offences for which divine justice has not yet inflicted a punishment, and for which you have not sufficiently expiated by a vol-

untary penance. When you see that God, in His infinite mercy, instead of a long punishment in purgatory, or even an eternal one in hell, has decreed but an easy and momentary one in this life, accept it, not merely with resignation, but with joyous thanksgiving.

3. If you think, without reason, that your faults are few, that you do a great amount of penance, remember that the road to heaven is narrow and full of obstacles.

4. Even if you could find another road, a burning love should prevent you from considering it; for the Son of God, and all the saints after Him, took no other road than the thorny path of the Cross.

5. What you should keep in mind at this and all other times is the will of God. He loves you so tenderly that He is delighted with every heroic act of virtue you perform and with the return of your fidelity and courage to His immense love. Remember also that the more unjustly you suffer, and consequently the more grievous your affliction, the greater is your merit in the sight of God. For in the midst of your suffering you adore His judgments, and willingly submit to His divine Providence which draws good from the greatest evil and makes the malice of our enemies subservient to our eternal happiness.

CHAPTER FIFTEEN

FURTHER ADVICE ON HOW TO FIGHT SKIL-
FULLY. THE ENEMIES WE ARE TO ENGAGE,
AND THE COURAGE NECESSARY TO FIGHT
THEM

YOU HAVE SEEN the conduct that must be observed
to gain the victory over self, and to attain the
necessary virtues. To do this with greater facility
and speed we must not be content with exhibiting
our courage but a single time. It is necessary to
return so often to the battle, particularly when
engaged with self-love, that at last we can judge
all those our friends from whom we receive the
most cruel and mortifying injuries. It frequently
happens that where this kind of combat is shirked
the victories are harder, very imperfect, less frequent, and soon lost again.

Fight, therefore, with great determination. Do
not let the weakness of your nature be an excuse.
If your strength fails you, ask more from God.
He will not refuse your request. Consider this—
if the fury of your enemies is great, and their
numbers overwhelming, the love which God holds
for you is infinitely greater. The angel who pro-
tects you and the saints who intercede for you are
more numerous.

There are many women who, through these
considerations, have baffled the wisdom of the

world, conquered the allurements of the flesh, triumphed over the malice of the devil.

Do not, therefore, lose heart, although you may think that it is a difficult task to absorb the attacks of so many enemies, that this warfare will continue your entire lifetime, and that inescapable ruin threatens you on all sides. But remember this—neither the power nor the trickery of your enemies can hurt you without the permission of Him for Whose honor you fight. He delights in this kind of battle and, as far as possible, encourages everyone to engage in it. But He is so far from permitting your enemies to accomplish their evil plans that He will fight on your side and sooner or later crown your endeavors with victory, though the battle may end only with your life.

All He asks of you is that you defend yourself courageously, and that, despite any wounds you may receive, you never lay down your arms or leave the battleground.

You must not shirk your duty. This war is unavoidable, and you must either fight or die. The obstinacy of your enemies is so fierce that peace and arbitration with them is utterly impossible.

CHAPTER SIXTEEN

THE SOLDIER OF CHRIST MUST PREPARE EARLY FOR THE BATTLE

THE FIRST THING to do when you awake is to open the windows of your soul. Consider yourself as on the field of battle, facing the enemy and bound by the iron-clad law—either fight or die.

Imagine the enemy before you, that particular vice or disorderly passion that you are trying to conquer—imagine this hideous opponent is about to overwhelm you. At the same time, picture at your right Jesus Christ, your Invincible Leader, accompanied by the Blessed Virgin, St. Joseph, whole companies of angels and saints, and particularly by the glorious Archangel Michael. At your left is Lucifer and his troops, ready to support the passion or vice you are fighting and resolved to do anything to cause your defeat.

Imagine your guardian angel thus spurring you on: "Today you must fight to conquer your enemy and anyone who tries to ruin you. Be courageous. Do not be afraid or cowardly. Christ your Captain is here with all the power of Heaven to protect you from the enemy, and to see that they never conquer you, either by brute power, or by trickery. Hold your ground! Do violence to yourself, no matter how painful it is. Call out for the help of Jesus and Mary and all the Saints. If you do this, you will be victorious."

It does not matter how weak you are—how strong the enemy may seem, either in number or in power. Do not be discouraged. The help you have from heaven is more powerful than all that hell can send to destroy the grace of God in your soul. God, the Creator and the Redeemer, is Almighty and more desirous of your salvation than the devil can be of your destruction.

Fight courageously, then, and do not neglect to mortify yourself. Continual war on your inordinate inclinations and vicious habits will gain the victory, acquire the kingdom of Heaven, and unite your soul to God forever.

Begin to fight immediately in the name of the Lord, armed with distrust of yourself, with confidence in God, in prayer, and with the correct use of the faculties of your soul. With these weapons, attack the enemy, that predominant passion you want to conquer, either by courageous resistance, repeated acts of the contrary virtue, or any means that heaven gives you to drive it out of your heart. Do not rest until it is conquered. Your endurance will be rewarded by the Supreme Judge, Who, with the entire Church triumphant, has witnessed your behaviour.

To repeat—you must not become tired of this war. Everyone must serve and please God. It is impossible to avoid this fight. If anyone flees, he is exposed to being wounded and even destroyed. By revolting against God and indulging in a life of sensuality with the world the difficulties are not lessened, because both body and soul suffer greatly when given to luxury and ambition.

There is a great lack of vision in one who does not avoid a great deal of trouble in this life, followed by endless agony in the next, and yet shirks small difficulties which will soon end in an eternity of happiness and the never ending enjoyment of God.

CHAPTER SEVENTEEN

THE METHOD OF FIGHTING YOUR PASSIONS AND VICES

IT IS VERY IMPORTANT to know the procedure that must be followed in fighting your passions and vices so that you will not run about blindly, and merely beat the air, as so many do. They lose all the fruits of their labor.

You must begin with recollection in order to know what thoughts and desires usually occupy your mind. You must know your dominant passion which must be singled out as your greatest enemy, the first to be attacked.

But, if your enemy, as a diverting movement, should attack at another point, you must move to the point that is the most threatened and then immediately return to your primary position.

CHAPTER EIGHTEEN

How to Curb the Sudden Impulses of Your Passions

If you are not able as yet to bear patiently the injuries, insults, and other disturbances of this life, you must harden yourself for this task by foresight and by preparing for their reception.

Having discovered the nature of the passion from which you suffer the most, you must consider what kind of persons you have to deal with, what places you are wont to visit. From this data, you can discover just what disturbances are likely to occur.

However, if any unforeseen accident should happen, although it is a tremendous advantage never to be unprepared for any mortification or trouble, we shall point out a way of greatly relieving it.

The moment you find that you are affected by some unforeseen, injurious circumstance, be on your guard. Do not lose your self-control. Raise your mind to God and regard the occurrence as a trial from heaven. Reflect that God Himself, gentle Father that He is, permits this only that you may be able to purify yourself still more and unite yourself more closely to Him. He is infinitely pleased when He sees you cheerfully undergo the greatest trials for His sake.

Then turn your thoughts to yourself. Reprimand your lack of courage in this way: "Coward! Why do you turn from a cross placed upon you not by an ordinary person, but by your Father Who is in heaven?" Then turning to this cross, accept it not only with submission but with joy saying: "O Cross, made for me from the beginning by divine Providence; Cross that the love of my crucified Jesus makes sweeter to me than the greatest of sensual pleasures, place me upon thee that I may be united to Him Who became my Redeemer when He died in your arms!"

But if you find that you have been influenced so greatly that you are incapable of elevating your mind to God, and that even your will is affected, stop the evil there. It does not matter what agitation may have been stirred up in your heart. Spare nothing to conquer it. Beg heaven for assistance with great fervor.

Of course, the surest way of checking these first impulses of improper desires is to endeavor to eliminate the cause beforehand. For example, if you see that, because of an excessive attachment to anything, you are angered whenever your inclinations are denied, break off that attachment and you will enjoy perfect peace.

If the uneasiness you feel does not come from a liking for some pleasure, but from a dislike of some person who seems disagreeable to you in every act he performs, the best cure for this disease is to endeavor to love this person, despite the antipathy you may feel. Do this, not only because he was created to the same image of God, and redeemed by the same Precious Blood of Christ as yourself, but also because by bearing patiently with certain defects you imitate your heavenly Father Whose love and goodness extends to all people without exception.

CHAPTER NINETEEN

How We Are to Fight Against Impurity

IN ENCOUNTERING THIS VICE we must use special tactics and greater resolution. In order to do this we must distinguish three phases of the operation —the first, which precedes the temptation—the second, during the temptation—the third, which follows the temptation.

1. Before the time of temptation we must avoid all persons and occasions that would expose us to sin. If it is necessary that we speak to such people, do it as speedily as possible; speak only on serious subjects with corresponding modesty and gravity. We must not permit the conversation to become familiar or frivolous.

Do not presume on your own strength despite the fact that after many years spent in the world you have remained firm against the force of concupiscence. For lust often achieves in one instant what whole years could not effect. Sometimes it will make long preparations for the assault. Then the wound is more dangerous when it comes least expected and under a disguise.

It must likewise be noted, and every day experience proves this, that the danger is always greatest on those occasion where there is the least appearance of evil. Here it is founded on the plausible pretences of friendship, gratitude, obligation, or on the merit and virtue of the persons involved. Impure inclinations imperceptibly insinuate themselves into such friendships through frequent visits, prolonged conversations, and indiscreet familiarities until the poison reaches the heart. The reason, then, is so blinded that it even connives at amorous glances, tender expressions, and facetious liberties in conversation which bring violent and almost irresistible temptations.

a. Be cautious—run away—you are more susceptible to occasions of this sin than straw is to fire. Do not rely on your own strength or on some resolution you have taken to die rather than of fend God. Despite your good intentions, frequent exciting conversations will enkindle a flame that cannot be extinguished. The impetuous desire of satisfying your passions will make you deaf to the warning of your friends. You will lose the fear of God, your reputation and even your life will be disregarded. Not even the fear of the flames of hell will be able to master the fury of the sensual fires enkindled in your heart. Look for safety, then, in flight. There is no other way to escape. Too much confidence will end in eternal destruction.

b. Avoid idleness. Determine what you have to do, and then fulfill exactly the duties of your position in life.

c. Obey your superiors promptly; do what they command. In the things that are most mortifying and opposed to your inclinations, be even more cheerful.

d. Never judge others rashly, particularly in regard to impurity. If any are unfortunate enough to fall into such disorder, and even if the affair becomes public, you must not treat them with scorn and contempt. Rather pity their weakness, and take advantage of the occasion to humble yourself before God, acknowledging that you are but dust and ashes. Redouble your prayers and avoid with greater care all dangerous company, however insignificant may be your reasons for suspecting it. For if you permit yourself the liberty of severe judgments on your neighbors, God will permit you, for your punishment and amendment, to fall into the same faults for which you condemned others, in order that by such humiliation you may discover your own pride and rashness, and then you can find proper remedies for both.

Although it is possible that you would avoid these degrading sins, yet be assured that, if you continue to form these rash judgments, you are in great danger of ruin.

e. If you discover that your heart is rich in spiritual comforts and joys, you must be on guard against a secret complacency with yourself, against imagining that you have attained perfection and that the enemy can no longer do you any harm because you apparently have nothing but scorn and contempt for him. The greatest caution is necessary here to prevent a relapse.

2. We come to an examination of the actual time of temptation. In the first place, we must

determine whether the cause of the temptation is exterior or interior.

By an exterior cause is meant curiosity of the eyes or ears to the point where decency suffers, vanity in one's dress, too tender friendships, and indiscreet familiarities. Modesty and decency are the proper remedies for this evil; they shut the eyes and ears to those things that cloud the imagination. The real remedy, as we have said, is to run away from all such occasions of sin.

Interior causes proceed from a pampered body, from many bad thoughts that come from evil habits or the suggestions of the devil. When the body has been pampered too much, it must be mortified by fasting, discipline, and other austerities which, however, must always be regulated by discretion and obedience.

From whatever source unchaste thoughts may arise, we can drive them away by serious application to our proper duties, and by prayer and meditation.

Your prayer should be conducted in the following manner. When you see these thoughts present themselves and attempt to make an impression, recollect yourself and speak to Christ crucified saying: "Sweet Jesus, come to my rescue, that I may not fall a victim to my enemies." On certain occasions you may embrace a crucifix representing your dying Saviour, kiss the marks of the Sacred Wounds on His feet and say with great confidence and affection: "O adorable, thrice holy Wounds! Imprint your figure on my heart which is filled with evil, and preserve me from consenting to sin."

In your meditations I am not of the opinion (as several authors are) that, when the temptation is most violent, you should consider the degrading and insatiable nature of these sins in order to establish a hatred for impurity, that you should consider how they are followed by disgust, remorse and anxiety, even by the loss of one's fortune, health, life, honor, etc. These considerations are not appropriate to the situation and, instead of freeing us from the danger, they frequently only increase it. If the understanding drives away evil thoughts, these reflections naturally call them back.

The best way to become free of these is to remove not only the thoughts themselves, but also the reflections directly contrary to them. In attempting to dissipate them by their contraries, we merely renew the impure ideas and unconsciously imprint them still deeper. Be satisfied with meditation on the life and death of our Saviour. If, while you are doing this, the same thoughts should return, even more disturbing than before, as may possibly happen, do not be discouraged or abandon your meditation, do not exert yourself in driving them away. Ignore and despise these miserable deceits of the devil and persist, with all possible attention, in your meditation on the death of our Saviour. Nothing can be more effective in putting your enemy to flight, despite his determination to resist.

Conclude your meditation with some prayer such as the following: "O My Creator and Redeemer, save me from my enemies through Thy infinite goodness and the merits of Thy bitter passion." But remember, when you say this do not think about the particular vice from which you are endeavoring to free yourself. The least reflection on it may be dangerous. Above all, do not waste any time disputing with yourself about how much you may have yielded to the temptation. Such scrutiny is an invention of the enemy, who under the deceiving appearance of an imaginary duty, attempts to renew the attack, or at least hopes to make some impression with the bad thoughts he had poured into your mind.

When, therefore, it is evident that you have consented to the evil, let it suffice to tell your spiritual director in a few words just what has occurred. Do just as he advises, and do not trouble yourself further with it.

You must be sure, however, not to conceal anything because of shame or any other reason. If humility is necessary to conquer our common enemies, it is infinitely more so in this case because this vice is, for the most part, a just punishment for pride.

3. After you have conquered the temptation, you should conduct yourself as follows. Although you enjoy complete peace and consider yourself safe, avoid with the greatest care all objects that tend to temptation. Exclude them completely from your mind, even if they seem to be virtuous

or good. These perversions are the illusions of a corrupt nature or traps laid by the devil, who would transform himself into an angel of light in order to drag you down with him into the darkness of Hell itself.

CHAPTER TWENTY

How to Combat Sloth

It is of the greatest importance to make war against sloth. This vice is not only an obstacle on our way to perfection, but it delivers us over to the enemies of our salvation. If you desire to fight this vice in earnest, begin by avoiding all curiosity and vain amusements. Withdraw your affections from worldly things and stop all pursuits that are not in harmony with your state of life.

Strive assiduously to comply with the inspirations of heaven, to execute the orders of your superiors, to do everything at the proper time and in the proper manner. Do not hesitate a moment in the execution of a command. The first delay brings on a second, this a third, and thus we lose ground. For the dread of labor and the love of ease increase in proportion to their indulgence. Labor becomes so distasteful that a lethargic hesitancy in applying oneself to work, or even the total neglect of work, is the result.

It is difficult to shake off the habit of sloth, once it is acquired, unless shame accompanies this indolent life and rouses us to greater diligence and application. Sloth, moreover, is a poison that spreads itself through all the faculties of the soul. It not only infects the will by making work odious to it, but also the understanding by so blinding it that the resolutions of the slothful usually have no effect. What should be done without delay is either neglected or deferred to some other time.

Mere swiftness of action, however, is not enough. Things must be done at the proper time, and in the most perfect manner possible. A precipitous act, which is done with no regard for its proper execution, but only to be rid of the trouble and to enjoy peace again as soon as possible, cannot be called diligent. It is rather an artful, refined sloth.

This disorder springs from a failure to consider the great value of a good work which is done at the proper time and in a correct manner. Such an act overcomes all the obstacles which sloth places before those who enter the battle against their vices.

Reflect frequently, therefore, that a single aspiration, an ejaculation, a genuflection, the least sign of respect for the Divine Majesty, is of greater value than all the treasures of the earth. Every time a person mortifies his inclinations, the angels present him with a crown of glory as a reward for the victory gained over himself.

On the contrary, God gradually withdraws His graces from those who neglect them, and increases the fervor of the diligent souls until, at length, He introduces them into the joys of heaven.

You may, at first, find your strength insufficient to undergo all the difficulties and troubles that you will encounter on your road to perfection. Then you must acquire the habit of hiding them

from yourself. They will appear more insignificant than the slothful are apt to imagine them
to be.

When an act must be repeated many times in
order to acquire some particular virtue, and this
has to be continued for several days in opposition
to countless powerful enemies, begin to do these
acts as though a few would suffice and your trouble
would soon end. Attack one enemy at a time, as
though you had but one to encounter. Be confident that, with God's grace, you will master them
all. In this way you will overcome your sloth and
acquire the contrary virtue.

Use the same method in regard to prayer. If
you are to pray for an hour, and the time seems
long, begin as though you were to pray but a
quarter of an hour. When that is finished, propose another quarter hour, and the hour will
elapse imperceptibly.

If, however, during this period you experience
a great repugnance and aversion to prayer, cease
praying for a while. In a short time return again
to the prayers that you had interrupted.

This is also true in regard to manual labor. If
you feel that you are overwhelmed by the amount
of work before you and by the difficulties involved, do not permit indolence to discourage
you. Begin with what demands your immediate
attention and do not think of the rest. Be very
diligent, for when this is well done, the remainder
will follow with much less trouble than you had
anticipated.

This is the way to face difficulties. Never hesitate to work. There is good reason to fear lest sloth should so triumph within you that even the first step towards virtue is made impossible, and a horror of work is imprinted on your mind before you have actually experienced the least difficulty in its accomplishment. This is what happens to weak, cowardly souls. They are in continual dread of the enemy, no matter how weak and remote from them he may be. They are ever apprehensive lest more should be laid upon them than they can bear. Consequently, they have no rest even when most at ease.

Realize, then, that in this vice there is a poison which not only chokes the first seeds of virtue, but even destroys those already formed. What the worm does in wood, sloth effects in the spiritual life. It is used very successfully by the devil to draw men into snares, particularly those who seek perfection.

Guard yourself, pray, and do good. Do not defer making your wedding garment until you are called upon to go forth and meet the Heavenly Bridegroom.

Reflect every day on the fact that He Who has granted you the morning has not promised the evening, and, should He grant this, He gives no assurance of the following morning. Spend each day, therefore, as if it were the last; cherish nothing but the will of God, for you will have to render a strict account for every moment.

A final observation should be made. Although

you have transacted a great deal of business and have undergone many hardships, you may consider the day worthless and your labor unprofitable, unless you have gained many victories over your passions and your own will, unless you have gratefully acknowledged the benefits received from God, particularly His death on the Cross, unless you have accepted as blessings whatever chastisements the Father of infinite mercy has inflicted as an expiation for your many sins.

CHAPTER TWENTY-ONE

THE PROPER USE OF OUR SENSES. HOW THEY MAY HELP US TO CONTEMPLATE DIVINE THINGS

ONE MUST GIVE great care and constant application to the correct regulation of his senses. The sensitive appetite, the source of all actions of our weakened nature, has an unquenchable thirst for pleasure. Since it cannot satisfy itself, it uses the senses to attract their proper objects and then transmits these images to the mind. Sensual pleasures, consequently, by reason of the union which subsists between body and soul, spread themselves through all the senses capable of pleasure and then seize, like a contagious disease, upon the spiritual faculties. In this way they effect the corruption of the entire man.

You can use the following remedies against this enormous evil. Watch your senses carefully. Use them only for some good purpose, some advantageous motive or real necessity, never for the sake of mere pleasure. If they do go astray, perhaps unnoticed, if they transgress the bounds which reason prescribes, check them immediately. They must be so regulated that, instead of embracing objects for the sake of false pleasure, they become accustomed to draw from the same objects great helps for the sanctification and perfection of the soul. The soul, then, through recollection is able to rise from the knowledge of earthly things to the contemplation of the divine goodness. This can be done in the following way.

When an agreeable object is presented to the senses, do not become absorbed in its material elements, but let the understanding judge it. If there is anything in it that does please the senses, remember that this is not from the thing itself, but from God, Whose invisible hand created and endowed it with all its goodness and beauty. Rejoice in the thought that this sovereign and independent Being is the sole Author of all the charming qualities that His creatures possess. He Himself possesses them all in a manner infinitely superior to the most excellent created beings.

In contemplating a beautiful work of creation consider that, in itself, it is nothing. Let your thoughts soar to the great Hand that produced it; place all your delight in Him saying: "O my God! Sole Object of my desires! Universal Source of all good things! How delightful it is to consider that the perfections of creatures are but a faint image of Thy glory!"

When you behold the verdant trees or plants and the beauty of flowers, remember that they possess life only through the will of that divine Wisdom that, unseen by all, gives life to all things. Say to Him: "O Living God! O Sovereign Life! Thou delight of my soul! From Thee, in Thee and through Thee all things on earth live and flourish!"

The sight of animals should lift your mind and heart to the Author of sensibility and motion. Say with respect and love: "Great God, Unmoved Mover of all things, how I rejoice when I consider the eternity of Thy existence, incapable of the slightest change!"

When the beauty of mankind impresses you, you should immediately distinguish what is apparent to the eye from what is seen only by the mind. You must remember that all corporeal beauty flows from an invisible principle, the uncreated beauty of God. You must discern in this an almost imperceptible drop issuing from an endless source, an immense ocean from which numberless perfections continually flow. How my soul is ravished when I consider that Eternal Beauty, the Source of every beautiful thing!

You must also distinguish, when you meet a person who is intelligent, just, affable, or gifted in any other way, just how much is his own and how much he has received from Heaven. Then will you exclaim: "O God of all virtue! I cannot express my joy when I consider that all good comes from Thee, and all the perfections of created beings are nothing when compared with Thee! Thank Thee for this and all good things bestowed on my neighbor or on myself. Have pity on my poverty and be mindful of the great need I have of such virtues!"

When you have performed a good act, recall that God is the author of the act, and you are but His instrument. Lift up your eyes to Him and cry out: "O Sovereign Lord of the universe! It is with the greatest pleasure that I recognize that, without Thee, the First and Principal Cause of all things, I can do nothing."

When you taste anything pleasant, consider that God alone is capable of giving it that taste which is so agreeable to you. Find all your delight in Him and say: "Rejoice, O my soul! Without God there is no true or substantial happiness!"

Do not be satisfied with the pleasure that comes from a pleasant scent. Mount in spirit to Heaven, and rejoice in God from Whom it came. Beg of Him that, being the Author of all sweetness, He will move your soul, freed from all sensual pleasure, to raise itself to Him as a fragrant perfume.

When you hear beautiful music, turn to God and exclaim: "O God! Thy divine perfections fill my heart with delight; their melodious harmony is infinitely pleasing not only to Thyself, but to angels, men and all created beings!"

CHAPTER TWENTY-TWO

How Sensible Things May Aid Us to Meditate on the Passion and Death of Our Saviour

It has been shown how we may rise from the consideration of sensible things to the contemplation of the greatness of God. Now we must learn how to relate these things to the memory of the sacred mysteries of Our Lord's life and death.

Everything in the world can be related to this end. Consider just the fact, as we have already suggested, that God is the First Cause of all things, that He has given to every creature, even the most exalted, its being, beauty, and all the perfections with which it is endowed. Then admire the infinite goodness of this Sovereign Master of the universe, Who condescended to become man, and suffer an ignoble death for your salvation. He even permitted His own creatures to plot against Him and to nail Him to the cross. If you want to enter into the details of His sufferings, everything about you will be a reminder of them.

Weapons, cords, thorns, reeds, nails, hammers, will readily bring to mind the instruments of His agony.

An humble cottage will represent the stable and manger where He was born. The rain falling on the earth will call to mind the bloody sweat with which He watered the Garden of Olives.

The stones are figures of the rocks which split at His death. When you gaze at the sun or the earth, remember that when He died the earth trembled, and the sun grew dark. The sight of water will recall the water flowing from His side. A thousand other objects will lend themselves to these considerations.

When you drink, think of the gall and vinegar which was offered as refreshment to our amiable Saviour by His enemies. If you take too much satisfaction in perfumes, consider the stench of the dead carcasses that greeted Him on Mount Calvary.

When dressing remember that the Son of God clothed Himself with our flesh, that we might be clothed with His divinity. In removing your clothes, think of Him, stripped at the hands of His executioners, about to be scourged and nailed to the Cross for your sake.

Any tumultuous din should recall the horrible cries of the enraged populace against their Lord: "Away with Him! Away with Him! Crucify Him! Crucify Him!"

Whenever the clock strikes, remember the anguished beats of the Sacred Heart of Jesus when, in the Garden of Olives, He contemplated His approaching Passion and Death. Or it may call to mind the strokes of the hammer with which the soldiers nailed Him to the Cross.

In brief, whatever you suffer yourself, or see others undergo, is far short of the pains of body and soul that your Saviour suffered during His Passion.

CHAPTER TWENTY-THREE

OTHER ADVANTAGEOUS USES OF THE SENSES IN DIFFERENT SITUATIONS

IT HAS BEEN POINTED OUT how one's mind may be elevated from the things of earth to those of heaven that it may contemplate the varied mysteries concerning Christ. I shall continue and point out other subjects of meditation that will serve to satisfy the devotion of persons of diverse tastes. This will not only prove useful to the beginner, but also to those who are more instructed and advanced in the spiritual life. All of these do not follow the same method in striving for perfection, nor are they equally capable of deep contemplation.

Do not think that a variety of methods will create difficulties. Let discretion be your guide. Take the advice of a prudent director and obey his directions with great humility. This applies not only to what I am considering here, but also to what I shall say later on.

A thing, attractive and esteemed by the world, should be regarded as more insignificant than the dirt under your feet. It falls infinitely short of what heaven promises, whither you should aspire with all your heart, despising the world's foolish interests.

When you look at the sun, think of your soul. Adorned with sanctifying grace, your soul is incomparably more resplendent and beautiful than the entire firmament—but destitute of it, it is blacker than hell itself. Lift up your heart, then, to heaven when you gaze at the sky. Establish your right to an eternal dwelling place by guarding the integrity of that grace.

When you hear the song of the birds, think of the harmonies that sing heaven's eternal hymn of praise to God, and beg the Master to make you worthy to join the heavenly choir in singing His praises throughout eternity.

The charm and beauty of creatures should not deceive your judgment. The serpent is often concealed under enchanting appearances, seeking to poison and destroy the very life of your soul. Your very wrath will speak out: "Depart, cursed serpent, it is in vain that you hide for my destruction!" Then you will turn to God and say: "Blessed art Thou, O God! Thou hast discovered my enemy. He sought to destroy me, and Thou hast saved me!"

Seek refuge in the wounds of your Crucified Saviour. Completely absorbed in them, consider the overwhelming sufferings that divinity itself endured to rescue you from sin and to inspire you with an aversion for sensual pleasures.

Here is another means of estimating the attractiveness of created beauty. Take into consideration the changes that death will make in what now appears so charming.

Each step a person takes is a reminder of the approach of death.

The swift flight of the bird, or the rushing torrent of a river, is slow when compared with the swiftness of human life.

A storm that destroys everything, a peal of thunder that shakes the earth, recall the day of judgment. They send us to our knees in adoration before God, beseeching Him to give us grace and sufficient time to prepare for our appearance before His infinite Majesty.

If you desire, however, to make use of the innumerable incidents which occur in this life, the following method may be practiced. The sufferings brought by the heat, or cold, or any other inconvenience, the heavy weight of grief or sorrow, may be considered as the eternal decrees of Providence which sends suffering for your own good and proportions it to your strength. In this way, God's fatherly love and tenderness for you will become evident. It is apparent in the opportunities that He gives you to serve Him in the way that is most pleasing to Him.

Now that you are in a position to please Him more than ever, speak from the fulness of your heart and say: "It is the will of God that is accomplished in me. From all eternity God's love has chosen me to undergo this suffering today. May He be blessed forever!"

A firm conviction that all good thoughts come from God will lead you to thank the Father of light whenever these occupy your mind.

The promptings and inspiration of the Holy Spirit are to be seen in any religious book that you read. In the cross you will see the banner of Jesus Christ, your Captain. Realize that if you leave Him for just a moment, your most cruel enemies will seize you, but if you follow Him, you will be received, emblazoned with the medals of the victor, into the kingdom of Heaven.

When you see a statue of the Blessed Virgin, offer your heart to that Mother of mercy. Rejoice that she always observed the will of God perfectly, that she brought forth the Saviour of the world and nourished Him with her milk. Thank her also for the favors and helps that she never refuses us in our spiritual combats.

The representations of the saints will remind you of those valiant soldiers of Christ who, fighting courageously till death, have marked the road you must follow to someday share in their glory.

Each time the bell rings for the Angelus, make a short reflection on the words that precede each Hail Mary.

The first consideration is thanksgiving to God for the message sent from heaven, which began the work of our redemption.

The second reflection is one of rejoicing with Mary because of the sublime dignity to which she was elevated by her own incomparably profound humility.

The third sound of the bell will recall to our minds the Word, now made Man. And then we shall acknowledge the honor due His Blessed

Mother and the Archangel Gabriel. A respectful inclination of the head is proper each time the bell is rung, but particularly at the third.

Now these are acts that may be performed at any time. Certain exercises which concern the mysteries of our Saviour's Passion, and are more adapted to particular times of the day, as morning, noon, and night, will be treated later. But we must also frequently recall the sorrows that our Blessed Mother endured at that time, for only ingratitude could lead us to forget them.

At night consider the deep affliction that chaste and delicate Virgin felt at the bloody sweat and the seizure of her son Jesus in the garden, and all the agonies of her mind throughout the entire night.

In the morning feel with her the sorrows she suffered when she saw her beloved Son dragged before Pilate and Herod, condemned to death, and burdened with a heavy Cross.

Noon will bring the picture of the sword of grief that pierced the soul of this afflicted mother when she saw Him crucified, dying, His side pierced by a cruel lance.

These reflections on the sorrows of the Blessed Virgin may be made from Friday evening to Saturday noon. The preceding meditations may be made at any time. External circumstances or certain occasions will suggest other things for your own particular devotion.

In conclusion, I offer a short resumé of the best means of regulating your senses. Never permit love or hatred to enter your heart on purely human motives. Rather let the will of God direct your inclinations to embrace or reject the objects presented to your mind.

You must be careful to note that, with regard to this great variety of practices recommended to regulate your senses, it is far from my intention that you should spend all of your time on them. Quite the contrary. Recollection and attachment to God should be your normal attitude. Your chief activity will be the interior conflict with your vicious inclinations and the performance of acts of the contrary virtues. These methods have been proposed that they may be used at the proper occasion.

It must not be imagined that a multiplicity of exercises will produce any real progress in devotion. Although they may be good in themselves, their improper use may only serve to confuse the mind, increase self-love and instability, and thus open a way to the illusions of the devil.

CHAPTER TWENTY-FOUR

How to Govern One's Speech

WE MUST GIVE careful attention to our speech because of our tendency to speak on anything that is attractive to our senses. This inclination is rooted in a certain pride. We think that we know a great deal about things and, fond of our own conceptions, we do not hesitate to communicate them to others. We think the entire assembly should be attentive to us.

One could not easily enumerate all the evil consequences arising from uncontrolled speech.

In general, we may say that it occasions much loss of time; it is a certain sign of ignorance and shallowness; it usually involves detractions and lies, and cools the fervor of devotion. It reinforces our disorderly passions, and establishes a habit of loose and idle talk.

As a method of correcting this, I would suggest the following. Do not talk too much!—either to those who do not readily listen to you, lest you bore them, or to those who enjoy hearing you, lest you be led into improper avenues of conversation.

Loud and dictatorial tones are not pleasing to the ear and only reveal your presumptuous ignorance.

One should speak of himself, of his accomplishments, of his relatives, only when compelled to do so. And then these should be discussed as briefly and modestly as possible. If you meet someone who talks only of himself, try to find a good reason to excuse him, but do not imitate him, though everything he says should serve only as an occasion for humiliation and self-accusation.

Speak willingly of God and His immense charity for us. But lest you fail to express yourself correctly, prefer to hear and treasure in your heart the words of others on this subject.

When worldly talk reaches your ears, do not let it touch your heart. If it is necessary for you to listen to it, to understand and comment on it, lift your heart to heaven. There reigns your God, and from thence that divine Majesty condescends to behold you, unworthy as you are. After you have decided what to say, eliminate some of it because, in the end, you will always discover that you have said too much.

Silence has a definite value in the spiritual warfare. Its observance is an assurance of victory. Generally speaking, it is accompanied by distrust of self and confidence in God, a greater desire for prayer, and facility in practicing virtue.

To arouse in yourself a love of silence consider the great advantages it offers and the numberless evils that spring from an unchecked loquacity. To become accustomed to infrequent speech, you should practice restraint even when you might be permitted to speak, unless this silence should be detrimental to yourself or to others.

Unprofitable discourse is to be avoided. The

company of God, His saints and angels, is to be preferred to that of man.

If you really have in mind at all times the war you have undertaken, you will hardly find time to breathe, much less to throw your energy away in silly, inane conversations.

CHAPTER TWENTY-FIVE

The Soldier of Christ, Resolved to Fight and Conquer His Enemies, Must Avoid, as Far as Possible, Anything That Intrudes Upon His Peace of Mind

OUR PEACE OF MIND when lost demands every possible exertion for its recovery. We actually never can lose it or cause it to be disturbed except through our own fault.

We must be sorry for our sins. But this sorrow must be calm and moderate. Our compassion for sinners and sadness at their destruction must be free of vexation and trouble, as it springs from a purely charitable motive.

The countless trials that crowd this life—sickness, wounds, death, the loss of friends and relatives, plagues, war, fire, etc., which men, naturally averse to suffering, dread—all these, through God's grace, may not only be received submissively from the hand of God, but can become occasions of joy. This is true if we view them as just punishments, inflicted on sinners, or as opportunities given the just to obtain merits.

These trials and events occur at the design of our Master; the severest tribulations of this life bring His will to our aid, so that we can march with a calm and tranquil soul. Any disquiet on our part is displeasing to God. For of whatever nature it may be it is always accompanied by some imperfection, and it always has a tendency towards self-love in one form or another.

Let there always be a vigilant sentinel in your soul which will discover anything that might trouble or disturb your conscience. At its first alarm, seize your weapons to defend yourself. Remember that all these evils, and a great many others, no matter how formidable their appearance, are but imaginary for they cannot deprive you of any real good. Consider this fact. Whether God decrees or permits these things for the reasons given above, or for others which we should certainly consider equitable, they are hidden from our comprehension.

You will find it greatly advantageous to preserve a calm mind through all the events in your life. Without it, your pious exercises will be fruitless.

I am convinced that, if the heart is troubled, the enemy is ever able to strike us, and as much as he wishes. Moreover, in that state we are not capable of discerning the true path to follow, the snares that must be avoided to attain virtue.

The enemy detests this peace. For he knows that this is the place where the spirit of God dwells, and that God now desires to accomplish great things in us. Consequently he employs his most devilish means to destroy this peace. He suggests various things that apparently are good. It is a trap; you will soon discover that these desires will destroy the peace of your heart.

As a remedy for this dangerous attack we must

be on guard against any new desire seeking entrance into our heart. Never permit its entrance until you have completely submerged your self-love in offering this to God. Confess your ignorance and beg God to clarify the matter and show you whether this desire comes from Him or our enemy. If possible, you should have recourse to your spiritual director.

Even when we are convinced that this action is prompted by the Holy Spirit we should, nevertheless, defer its execution until our eagerness to do this has been mortified. Preceded by such a mortification a good work is more pleasing to God than when it is pursued too impetuously. It frequently happens that the performance of the act brings less merit than the mortification.

Through the rejection of evil desires, and the suspension of even the good ones until we have suppressed the motivations of self-love, we shall preserve perfect tranquillity of mind.

It is also necessary to overcome a certain interior regret. Apparently coming from God, under the guise of remorse of conscience for past sins, it is, without doubt, the work of the devil. The following test will clearly point this out.

Whenever this regret produces greater humility, when it increases our fervor in doing good works and our confidence in the Divine Mercy, we must receive it in a spirit of gratitude as a gift from heaven. But when it occasions anxiety, when it makes us disconsolate, slothful, fearful and slow to do our duty, we may certainly conclude that it has been suggested by the enemy, and should be disregarded.

It frequently happens, moreover, that our anxieties arise from the trials of this life. There are two preservatives against them.

First. The consequences of these trials must be considered. They may completely destroy our desire of attaining perfection, or they may destroy our self-love. The diminution of self-love, one of our greatest enemies, gives no cause for complaint. Such trials should be received with joyful thanksgiving as favors bestowed by God. If they incline us to swerve from the path of perfection, and make virtue repugnant, we must not be downhearted and lose our peace of mind. This will be considered later.

Second. Let us raise our hearts to God. Whatever He wills, without exception, should be received with the firm persuasion that every cross He wills to send shall prove an endless source of blessing, a treasure whose value one may not appreciate at the moment.

CHAPTER TWENTY-SIX

What We are to do When Wounded

When you realize that you have been wounded by sin, whether through weakness or malice, do not lose your courage or become panic-stricken. Turn to God with a great and humble confidence saying: "See, O Master, what I am able to do. When I rely on my own strength, I commit nothing but sins."

Meditating on this, recognize the extent of your humiliation and express to our Lord your sorrow for the offence committed. With an unperturbed heart, indict your vicious passions, especially the one that has occasioned your fall, and confess: "O Lord, I would not have stopped at this had not Your goodness restrained me."

Give thanks to God, and more than ever give to Him the complete love of your heart. What generosity on His part! You have offended Him and, despite this, He extends His hand to prevent another fall.

With your heart full of confidence in His infinite mercy, say to Him: "O Master, show forth Thy Divinity and pardon me! Never permit me to be separated from Thee, deprived of Thy help; never permit me to offend Thee again!"

After you have done this, do not upset yourself

by examining whether God has forgiven you or not. This is a complete loss of time, an outcropping of pride, a spiritual sickness, an illusion of the devil who seeks to harm you under cover of an apparently good act. Place yourself in the merciful arms of God, and plunge into your usual duties, as though nothing had happened.

The number of times during the day that you fall cannot shake the basis of a true confidence in Him. Return after your second, your third, your last defeat, with the same confidence. Each lapse will teach you greater contempt for your own strength, greater hatred for sin, and, at the same time, will give you greater prudence.

This will dismay your enemy because it is pleasing to God. The devil will be thrown into confusion, baffled by one he has so often overcome. As a result, he will bend every effort to induce you to change your tactics. He frequently succeeds when a strict watch is not kept over the tendencies of the heart.

The efforts expended in conquering yourself must correspond to the difficulties encountered. A single performance of this exercise is not sufficient. It should be frequently repeated though but one fault has been committed.

Consequently, if you have fallen, if you are greatly perturbed and your confidence is shaken, you must first recover your peace of mind and confidence in God. Raise your heart to heaven. Be convinced that the trouble that sometimes follows the commission of a fault is not so much a sorrow for having offended God, but is a fear of punishment.

The way to recover this peace is to forget, for the moment, your fault and to concentrate on the ineffable goodness of God and His burning desire to pardon the gravest sinners. He uses every possible means to call the sinners back, to unite them entirely to Himself, to sanctify them in this life, and make them eternally happy in the next.

This consideration, or others of its kind, will bring peace back to your soul. Then you may reconsider the malice of your error in the light of what has been said above.

Finally, when you approach the sacrament of Penance—I advise you to do this frequently—recall all of your sins and sincerely confess them. Reawaken your sorrow for having committed them, and renew your resolutions to amend your life in the future.

CHAPTER TWENTY-SEVEN

THE METHODS USED BY THE DEVIL TO TEMPT AND SEDUCE THOSE WHO DESIRE TO ACQUIRE VIRTUE, AND THOSE WHO ARE STILL THE PRISONERS OF VICE

MY BELOVED SON, never forget that the devil continually seeks your destruction. But his attacks against each soul are varied.

Before introducing you to some of his stratagems, we shall consider different types of persons in different situations.

There are some who are so overwhelmed by their sins that they never even consider the possibility of breaking their chains. Others want to free themselves from this slavery, but they do nothing to accomplish this. Some think they are secure, and for that very reason are very far from being so. Others, after attaining a high degree of virtue, fall all the more heavily. In the following chapters these various types will be treated.

CHAPTER TWENTY-EIGHT

THE CUNNING DEVICES USED BY THE DEVIL TO DESTROY COMPLETELY THOSE HE HAS ALREADY DRAWN INTO SIN

WHEN THE DEVIL has enmeshed the soul in sin, he uses every means at his disposal to distract its attention from anything that would enable it to recognize the terrible condition into which it has fallen.

The devil is not content to stifle every inspiration from Heaven, and to suggest evil thoughts in their place. He endeavours to plunge it into new faults, either of the same or a more vicious nature by supplying dangerous opportunities to sin.

Thus the soul, deprived of heavenly guidance, heaps sin upon sin, and hardens itself in its evil ways. Floundering in the mire, it rushes from darkness to darkness, from one pit to another, always moving farther from the path of salvation and multiplying sin upon sin, unless strengthened by an extraordinary grace from heaven.

The most efficacious remedy against this evil is the willing reception of the divine helps that will draw the soul from darkness to light, from vice to virtue. Let the soul cry out: "Lord, help me! Hasten to my relief! Do not leave me any longer in the darkness of sin and death!" Similar ejaculations should be frequently repeated.

If it is possible, one should immediately seek the advice of his confessor against the assaults of the enemy. If this is impossible, one should kneel before a crucifix, or beseech the Queen of Heaven for compassion and assistance.

Victory depends entirely on the diligent effort that is expended.

CHAPTER TWENTY-NINE

The Efforts of the Devil to Prevent the
Conversion of Those Who, Knowing the
Diseased Character of Their Souls, De-
sire to Amend Their Lives. The Reason
Why Their Good Intentions are Fre-
quently Ineffectual

THOSE WHO ARE COGNIZANT of the diseased character of their souls and desire to cure them are
often deluded by the devil. He endeavors to persuade them that they have a long time to live, and
consequently may safely defer their conversion.

He insinuates the impression that some business affair or difficulty must be cleared up before
they can devote themselves sufficiently to the spiritual life and fulfill its duties without disturbance.
This snare has entangled and daily does entangle
many. But its success is directly attributable to
their own supine neglect of a matter in which the
glory of God and their own salvation should be
the only considerations.

Let persons of this type say: "Now! Now!" instead of "Tomorrow! Tomorrow!" Why tomorrow? How can I be sure of living until it comes?
And even if I were, would I really be trying to
save my soul if I delayed my repentance? Would
it look as though I sought victory if I exposed
myself to fresh wounds?

It is beyond all dispute that a willing co-operation with the graces of heaven is the only way of escaping this delusion, together with the methods suggested in the preceding chapter. When I say "willing co-operation" I do not mean mere desires, or feeble and sterile resolutions, by which so many are deceived. The following are the reasons.

First. The foundation for such desires and resolutions is not mistrust of one's own abilities and confidence in God. The result is that a soul, inflated with secret pride, is so blind that it takes for solid virtue what is a mere illusion. The remedy for this evil, and the acumen necessary to recognize it, must be obtained from heaven which permits us to fall. This is done that our eyes may be opened by sad experience, that we may reassign the confidence we had in ourselves to divine grace, and that we may exchange an almost imperceptible pride for an humble knowledge of our own weakness. Good resolutions will never be effectual unless they are firm and steady, and they will never be firm and steady unless they are founded on a mistrust of one's own strength and on confidence in God.

Second. When we make a good resolution, we merely consider the beauty and excellence of virtue, which attracts even the most vapid minds, but we never consider the difficulties of attaining it. Consequently, cowardly souls are dismayed at the first sign of trouble and they hurriedly abandon their project. For this reason, it would be better for you to consider the difficulties which occur in acquiring virtue, rather than the virtues themselves, and to prepare yourself accordingly. You may rest assured that the greater courage you show in conquering yourself or defeating your enemies, the sooner will your difficulties diminish, and they will gradually vanish.

Third. We are too concerned with our personal advantage, rather than with virtue and adherence to the will of God. This frequently happens when we are comforted by the consolations we receive in a time of affliction. Finding that the comforts of the world have escaped us, we resolve to dedicate ourselves to God's service.

To be free of this charge, let us be careful not to misuse the grace of God. Let us be humble and prudent in forming good resolutions. Let us not seek extraordinary favors through rash promises which are beyond our capacities to fulfill.

If we are burdened with affliction, let us merely ask to carry our Cross as we should, since it comes from God. Let this be our glory, and we shall seek no alleviation from earth, or heaven itself. Let us ask, let us implore only that God may strengthen us in our trial, and that we may patiently undergo the trials He sees fit to send.

CHAPTER THIRTY

CONCERNING THE DELUSIONS OF SOME WHO CONSIDER THEMSELVES ON THE WAY TO PERFECTION

THE FRUSTRATION of the enemy in his first and second attacks will not discourage him from trying again to bring about your ruin. He would have you unconscious of your actual vices and passions, filling your imagination with visions of a chimerical perfection which he knows you will never attain.

Because of this subtle deception, we receive frequent and dangerous setbacks without giving much thought to means of countering them. Secret pride has seized upon these fanciful desires, mistaking the dream for the reality, and we rest in exalted notions of our own sanctity. Therefore, at the very time when the least contradiction or affront upsets us, we amuse ourselves with grandiose dreams of being ready to suffer the greatest torments or the pains of Purgatory itself for the love of God.

Our deception consists in the tendency of our sensitive nature (serenely comfortable when sufferings are at a distance), boldly to compare itself with those stalwart souls who bear the greatest pains with unwearied patience. To avoid such a snare, we must fight the enemies at hand in a world of reality, rather than achieve meaningless victories in a self-created world of fancy. Then we shall see if our resolutions are cowardly or courageous, imaginary or real, and thus advance to perfection in the footsteps of the saints.

We need not concern ourselves with those enemies who rarely molest us, unless we have reason to expect an attack from them, in which case we must be fortified with the soldier's resolve to conquer.

But let us not mistake resolutions for victories, even though we have made considerable progress in acts of virtue. True humility should accompany us with the ever-present memory of our weakness, bidding us put our confidence in God alone. Let us beseech Him to be our strength in the battle, our shield in danger, and our protection against presumption and confidence in our own abilities.

This is our path to greatness and perfection, a path along which we may find many difficulties for our frail natures that we may thereby be humbled and preserve the little reward our good work has already merited.

CHAPTER THIRTY-ONE

CONCERNING THE ARTIFICES EMPLOYED BY THE DEVIL TO MAKE US FORSAKE THE VIRTUOUS LIFE

THE FOURTH ARTIFICE which the devil employs on those who are advancing in the way of perfection is to fill them with ill-timed resolutions which in different circumstances would be quite commendable, but in the existing condition only engender vicious habits.

For example: a sick person bears his illness with such resignation that the enemy fears he will acquire habitual patience, and suggests to the victim the many creditable works he might do were he in a state of health. The victim is persuaded that his would be a service to God, humanity, and to his own soul were he physically well, and soon the enemy contrives to make him desirous of health and uneasy under his burden. The more earnest the wish, the greater the disappointment, and patience at length gives way to impatience under a burden that is viewed as hindering the accomplishment of works most acceptable to God.

Once the enemy has gained his point, the grand designs vanish gradually, and the patient is left with a gnawing dissatisfaction, and all the attendant evils arising from an impatient desire to cast off a yoke. Thus, what once promised to be a source of habitual virtue has become a source of a lamentable vice.

Such a delusion can be dispelled by exercising caution in the formation of pious designs incompatible with the state of suffering with which you are visited. For here ambition overreaches itself and leaves only anxiety and vexation.

Be mindful, in humility and resignation, that all of the benevolent aims you now have may not be carried out for want of courage once God has made you equal to their execution. At least you must consider the possibility of God's denying you the satisfaction of doing a good work, either by a hidden disposition of divine Providence, or as an atonement for past offences; perhaps in His wisdom, He wishes to see your human will attuned to His divine will, and see you humbled in spirit before omnipotence itself.

Show the same resignation when, either under the direction of your confessor, or for some other reason, you are obliged to refrain for a time from Holy Communion. Rather than be disturbed by this loss, you should say within your heart: "Were I not guilty of some failing or shortcoming before the Lord I would not be thus deprived of receiving Him; blessed be the name of Him Who has revealed to me my true unworthiness. I know, O Lord, that in all the trials of my life I need do nothing but bear them patiently in the hope of pleasing Thee, offering to Thee a heart conformable to Thy holy will. I know that in giving my heart to Thee it will be nourished in divine

consolation and fortified from the ever-threaten-
ing powers of hell. O Creator and Redeemer! Do
with me as thou wilt—may Thy will be my
strength, now and forever! All I ask is a cleansed
and virtuous soul, worthy of receiving Thee, and
desirious of executing Thy every wish!"

Those who assiduously follow these counsels
may be assured that, although they undertake a
work of piety far beyond their capacities, they will
nevertheless advance in the way of salvation and
in the way of serving God in the most acceptable
manner. This is true devotion. Even though the
motivation in this case be a device of the devil to
breed repugnance for virtue, or inspired by
heaven to test obedience, it still can prove ultimately beneficial to the soul.

We must exercise considerable caution, however, in employing certain means utilized by the
saints for eliminating troublesome infirmities, as
we are often too eager for the success of these
measures. Again, we must be utterly resigned,
proposing nothing to ourselves but the holy will
of God. For who of us can read in the mind of
God His solution to our individual problems? If
you rashly presume to improve on the divine plan,
you will be the sufferer. For impatience will
follow your consequent disappointment, and even
if you do not actually manifest impatience, you
have already lost that resignation that renders
your acts meritorious in the sight of God.

One cannot overlook at this point, a secret artifice of self-love which adroitly camouflages, as it

were, even the most blatant imperfections. A sick person, for instance, believes that his impatience springs from a just cause; that is, rather than impatience properly speaking, his uneasiness is to him a commendable regret for his faults which incurred the punishment of illness, or a just regret for the inconvenience he causes those who tend him.

The ambitious man who laments his failure to obtain a cherished position behaves similarly. He would be shocked were one to attribute his lamentations to vanity, and he protests his commendable motive, which he well knows would influence him little in different circumstances. Likewise the sick man who pretends so much uneasiness on account of the inconvenience caused those who tend him is no sooner well than he loses his solicitude for the suffering of his attendants at the hands of others. Obviously his impatience is not a glowing tribute to his sympathy for others, but rather an actual indictment of his love for himself.

And thus we advert again to the patient acceptance of the crosses of life which like a thread must be woven into the fabric of our spiritual lives.

CHAPTER THIRTY-TWO

The Last Artifice of the Devil in Making Even the Practice of Virtue an Occasion of Sin

THE EVIL ONE even uses virtue to tempt us to sin, inflating our egos with exaggerated self-esteem and complacency to the point where we succumb to vainglory. Thus we must be ceaselessly vigilant, cognizant of our own nothingness, our sinfulness, our appalling inadequacy, and ever mindful that we deserve nothing but eternal perdition. Let this remembrance be to us as a sword with which we defend ourselves from the insidious attacks of presumption and vanity; and let us fight with the vigor of a man struggling for his very life.

If, however, we desire a more perfect self-knowledge, let us distinguish between what we owe to the grace of God, and what we have merited ourselves. Let us recall the benevolence of God in endowing us with being, the mercy of God which sustains us, and the power of God which constantly preserves us. Unquestionably, therefore, those things which we truly merit of our own power are scarcely worthy of self-esteem, let alone the esteem of others. For our glories can be traced to heaven, but our sinfulness can be traced to ourselves.

Were we actually to compute the nature, number, and frequency of our offences—let alone the possible commission of faults prevented by the grace of God—we would find that cumulatively our vices are innumerable and our guilt equal to that of devils. Such considerations ought daily to bring to us the increasing realization of our own lowliness, and the gratitude we owe to divine goodness.

We must also be cautious to avoid vainglory, adhering strictly to the facts in self-scrutiny and self-judgment. For, although we are conscious of our wretchedness, if we wish the world to look upon us as saints, we deserve a criminal's punishment.

In order that you may be fortified against vainglory and rendered pleasing to Him Who is humility itself, it does not suffice that you have a lowly opinion of yourself, thinking yourself unworthy of good but deserving evil. Rather you must be willing to be despised, loath to accept praise, and eager to accept contempt, being certain, however, that true humility and not a stubborn haughtiness be your real motive. For subtle arrogance masquerades as Christian courage, despising the wisdom of the world and its judgment.

If anyone should show affection for you or commend your God-given qualifications, you must immediately be mindful of truth and justice, saying in your heart with all sincerity: "May I never, O Lord, attempt to rob Thee of Thy glory by attributing to myself that which is entirely owing to Thy holy grace! May honor and praise be Thine; may shame and confusion be mine!"

Regarding him who has praised you, be careful to scrutinize his motives, wondering what perfection he can discern in you. For God alone is good, and His works alone are laudable. Why indeed should man attempt to rest in a stolen glory?

Similarly, if you are lulled into a vain complacency by the remembrance of a good work, remember it was the grace of God in you bringing good out of your worthlessness. God alone is the author; God alone is deserving of praise.

Next consider, not the objective accomplishment of a good work, but the proportion between the grace given to perform that task and the result. Perhaps besides the innate deficiencies of the seemingly good work, a lack of fervor and deficiencies of intention and diligence further vitiate the act itself. Rather than bask in self-adulation, you should be grieved at your inadequate use of so much grace.

If you would compare your action to the saints, you would blush at the difference; if you compare your actions to the sublime immolation on Calvary's hill, they fade into utter insignificance. For Christ's life was a cross, the constant sacrifice of infinite dignity to human indignities, and the offering of purest love for those who gave Him naught but hate.

Lastly, if you raise your eyes to heaven and contemplate the majesty of God, then your puny deeds should make you ever fearful rather than proud, and make you utter in your heart with profound humility: "Lord, be merciful to me a sinner."

Be not prone to publish the favors received from God, as this is generally displeasing to Him, as might be seen from the following example. Appearing one day to a great saint in the guise of an infant, Christ was asked to recite the Hail Mary, and immediately started it. But having said "Blessed art thou amongst women" He was reluctant to sound His own praises, and when persuaded to do so, He disappeared. The devout soul, replenished with consolation, forever treasured this divine example of the importance of humility.

We must constantly endeavor, moreover, to humble ourselves in all of our actions which are but representations to the world of our nothingness. For in this humility is found the basis of innumerable other virtues. Just as God created our first parents out of nothing, so He continues to build our spiritual lives on our realization of the truth that we are nothing. Therefore the lower we humble ourselves, the higher the edifice rises; and in proportion to our progression into the depths of humility does the sovereign architect erect the structure to the heights of holiness. We can never too strongly emphasize this quest for self-abasement. O heavenly knowledge which gladdens us now and glorifies us hereafter! O admirable light piercing the darkness to enlighten our souls and raise our hearts to God! O precious but unknown jewel which gleams through the shadows of our sins!

This is an inexhaustible subject which could be developed to endless length. Whoever desires to honor the divine Majesty must rid himself of self-esteem and the desire of the esteem of others. Humble yourself before everyone, casting yourself at the feet of mankind if you sincerely wish God to be glorified in you and you in Him. To unite yourself with Him you must flee all grandeur, as He flees from those who constantly extol themselves. Choose the lowest place if you would have Him step down from the highest to embrace you with greater love. Choose the neglect of men that you may have the love of God.

Always render due thanks to Him, Who came to be despised on earth that you may be loved in heaven. Your thanks must go also to them who persecute you and are hostile to you, and you must be careful not to complain against them.

But if, despite all of these considerations, through the malice of Satan, lack of self-knowledge, or a propensity to arrogance, you are inflated with a supposed superiority, you must humble yourself the more as it is indicative of the little progress you have actually made, and the difficulty of overcoming the habit of pride. For humility will take the sting from the bite, change the poison to antidote, the evil into its proper remedy.

CHAPTER THIRTY-THREE

Some Important Instructions for Those Who Wish to Mortify Their Passions and Attain the Necessary Virtues

Although the method of subduing passions and acquiring the necessary virtues has already been treated at some length, there yet remains several instructions equal in importance to those already given.

1. If you desire to attain solid virtue and complete mastery over self, dividing the exercise of different virtues so as to assign particular virtues to particular days is to be avoided, resulting as it does in a state of perpetual vicissitude. The method that should be adopted seeks to root out the most predominant passions, striving the while to cultivate to an eminent degree the contrary virtue. For being once possessed of so essential a virtue, the rest may be acquired with less difficulty, as but few acts will be required for that end. And indeed so integral is the connection of one virtue with another, that whoever possesses one in its entirety, possesses all.

2. You must never set a definite time for the acquisition of any one virtue, specifying so many days, weeks, or years; rather like a vigorous soldier combating an unseen enemy, you must fight without ceasing until by a complete victory, the way to perfection is won. Every moment should be an

advance on the way to heaven, and every one who stops, rather than gaining breath and rest, loses both ground and courage. The advice to advance continually is meant to safeguard you from imagining you have reached the height of perfections, to encourage you to seize every opportunity to exercise new acts of virtue, and to preserve to the highest degree, a horror for sin.

In order that this may be accomplished, every duty must be performed with the greatest fervor and exactness, and you must on all occasions be habituated to the practice of every virtue. Embrace, therefore, any opportunity of advancing towards perfection and sanctity, especially such as are difficult; for such efforts are most effective in forming virtuous habits in the soul within a short time. And love those who furnish you with such opportunities, exercising caution at the same time as regards that which may be in the least prejudicial to chastity.

3. Considerable prudence and moderation are to be practiced in regard to the exercise of certain virtue which may prove deleterious to health. Such are severe discipline, hair shirts, fasting, long meditations and similar indiscreet penitential works. Rather than to be pursued too eagerly, the practice of exterior virtues must be a step by step process. On the other hand, the interior virtues such as the love of God, a hatred of the world, self-contempt, contrition for sin, mildness and patience, charity for enemies, know no bounds and should be practiced in the most eminent degree.

4. Let the culmination of all your plans and endeavors be the submission of the passion with which you are engaged, regarding such a victory as of the greatest consequence to you and the most acceptable to God. Eating or fasting, working or resting, at home or abroad, contemplative or active, let your aim be the conquest of that predominant passion and the acquisition of the contrary virtue.

5. Shun the luxuries and pleasures of life and the attacks of vice will be enfeebled, their force being drawn from the love of pleasure. But if you indulge in one sensual satisfaction while shunning another, if your war is against but one vice, be assured that although your wounds may not be grievous, the encounter will be sharp and the victory doubtful.

Keep, therefore, the words of Holy Scripture before your eyes: "He who loves his life, loses it; and he who hates his life in this world, keeps it unto life everlasting" (John 12, 25). "Therefore, brethren, we are debtors, not to the flesh, that we should live according to the flesh, for if you live according to the flesh you will die, but if by the spirit you put to death the deeds of the flesh, you will live" (Rom. 8, 12).

6. I conclude with a parting admonition to make what, if not necessary, is most salutary, viz., a general confession, with the requisite dispositions, that you may secure a perfect reconciliation with God, the Source of all graces, the Giver of victories, and the Dispenser of crowns.

CHAPTER THIRTY-FOUR

VIRTUES ARE TO BE ACQUIRED ONE AT A TIME AND BY DEGREES

ALTHOUGH A TRUE SERVANT of Jesus Christ, aspiring to the heights of perfection, should set no limits to his spiritual advancement, he should nevertheless exercise prudence as regards those excesses of fervor to which he is prone, and which at first seem feasible. For first fervor is apt to cool and may be entirely extinguished. It must be seen then, that besides the methods we have advocated with regard to exterior exercises, interior virtues too cannot be acquired but by degrees. For the foundations of a solid and lasting piety must be laid painstakingly, after which in a short time we may expect to make considerable progress.

For example, you must not attempt to acquire patience by immediately seeking crosses in which to delight; rather seek first the lowest degrees of this great virtue. Similarly, do not aim at all sorts of virtue—nor even many—simultaneously, but cultivate one firmly, then another, if you wish such habits to take deep root in your soul with greater facility. For in the acquisition of a particular virtue, and in the focusing of thought upon its cultivation, the memory will be exercised more in this one line of endeavor; your understanding, enlightened by divine assistance, will find new means and stronger motives for attaining it, and the will itself will be invigorated with fresh ardor in the pursuit. Such concentrated power of action is not possible when the three faculties are divided, as it were, by different objects.

Also, the acts necessary for the formation of the virtuous habit, mutually assisting each other to the same end, will be attended with much less difficulty as the latter acts make a deep impression on the heart, already suitably predisposed by the former ones.

The cogency of these reasons will appeal to you more forcibly if you reflect that anyone strenuously engaged in the pursuit of any one virtue, unconsciously advances in the practice of the rest. Moreover, the attainment of any one to an eminent degree inevitably introduces a great perfection to the others as they are, like the rays of the sun, almost inseparably united.

CHAPTER THIRTY-FIVE

The Most Profitable Means of Acquiring Virtue, and the Manner in Which We Apply Ourselves to a Particular Virtue for a Time

To the previous admonitions, I must add, that in order to attain solid piety, dauntless courage and a resolute will are absolutely indispensable where innumerable difficulties and contradictions are to be encountered. Also necessary is a particular fondness for the virtue, which arises from the frequent reflection that it pleases God, is admirable in itself, and is important to man. Furthermore, it is in virtue that all Christian perfection begins and ends.

It will be most important to resolve every morning upon a strict compliance to the virtue's dictates throughout the day, frequently examining how such resolutions have been put in practice. This formula is directed to the cultivation of that virtue which is the object of our immediate pursuit, and of which we are most in need. To this virtue must be referred all reflections drawn from the examples of the Saints, and our meditations on the life and death of our Saviour, which will be of infinite service in this spiritual warfare.

Let us accustom ourselves to the practice of both exterior and interior virtues that we may find the same ease and satisfaction in virtue that we find in obeying the tendencies of our corrupt nature. The acts most contrary to these corrupt tendencies are the most conducive to the establishment of habitual virtue in our souls.

Certain portions of Sacred Scripture, attentively pronounced or reverently considered, are similarly of great efficacy. Consequently, we should be familiar with those texts corresponding to the virtue in question, and employ them frequently, particularly when beset by the predominant opposite passion. Those, for instance, who strive to attain mildness and patience may repeat these or similar passages:

> "Bear patiently the wrath of God which comes upon you in punishment for your sins." Baruch 4:25.

> "The patience of the poor shall not perish, or be deprived of its reward." Psalms 9:19.

> "The patient man is better than the valiant; and he that ruleth his spirit, than he that taketh cities." Proverbs 16:32.

> "By your patience you will win your souls." Luke 21:19.

> "With patience run to the fight set before us." Hebrews 12:1.

These or similar aspirations may be used. O My God, when shall I be armed with patience as a shield against the weapons of my enemy? When shall I so love Thee as to receive with joy all the afflictions Thou shalt be pleased to send? O life of my soul, shall I never begin to live for Thy glory alone, perfectly resigned to all sufferings? O how happy should I be, if in the fiery trial of tribulation, I burn with a desire of being consumed for Thy service.

Let such prayers be offered frequently, as our devotion suggests, and our progress in virtue requires. They are called ejaculations, which like darts of fire directed to Heaven, lift our hearts heavenwards to the divine Goodness, when accompanied by two qualities which serve as wings: the one quality, a conviction of the delight God takes in seeing us labor for the cultivation of virtues; the other, an earnest desire of excelling in all virtue, for the sole motive of pleasing Him.

CHAPTER THIRTY-SIX

The Practice of Virtue Requires Constant Application

OF ALL THE THINGS conducive to the attainment of our present goal, viz., the acquisition of Christian virtues, the earnest desire of continual advancement is of the utmost importance, as the least pause retards us.

The moment we cease forming acts of virtue, our inclinations, naturally prone to ease and pleasures of the senses, raise in us disordered appetites which overthrow or at least weaken our virtuous habits. This is to say nothing of the loss, through such neglect, of countless graces which we might have merited by a constant application to our spiritual advancement.

This is the difference between a journey on earth, and that which leads to heaven. For in the former, not only may we stop without fear of going backward, but rest is necessary that we may sustain our strength to the journey's end; however, in the latter journey which leads to perfection, our growth in strength is proportionate to our advance, inasmuch as the inferior appetites which throw all possible obstacles in our path to heaven, grow gradually weaker while our good inclinations acquire new strength.

Thus as we advance in piety, our early difficulties fade into the background, and a certain delight, with which God sweetens the bitterness of this life, increases in our souls. Going cheerfully on from virtue to virtue, we finally reach the summit of the mountain, the summit of perfection, that happy state wherein the soul practices virtue, not only without revulsion, but with an effortless ease and ineffable pleasure. For triumphant over her passions, the world, and herself, she lives in God, and through Him, enjoys a peaceful serenity amid her continual labors.

CHAPTER THIRTY-SEVEN

CONCERNING THE NECESSITY OF SEIZING
EAGERLY ALL OPPORTUNITIES OF PRAC-
TICING VIRTUE SINCE OUR PROGRESS MUST
BE CONSTANT

WE HAVE ALREADY shown that the journey to perfection must be marked with continual advancement. Be vigilant, therefore, that you overlook no
opportunity of acquiring a virtue, and sedulously
guard yourself against the common fault of avoiding what is contrary to the inordinate affections of
our nature, since it is by combating them that we
rise to heroic virtues.

Using the same example to illustrate the acquisition of the virtue of patience—never avoid
the persons, the business, not even the thoughts
which to you have been the sources of much impatience. Rather accustom yourself to the person
you find most disagreeable, and to the task you
find most irksome, for there is no other way of
acquiring habitual patience.

If any employment, by its very nature, its author, or its contrariety to your inclinations, is the
source of personal discomfort, be sure not to give
it up on any of these accounts; show your courage,
not only in cheerfully accepting the situation, but
in persevering in it despite the vexations that

arise and the satisfaction you would derive in quitting it.

The same may be said of thoughts which are particularly irksome. No advantage is derived in being entirely freed from them, for the uneasiness they create will gradually inure you to bear the most vexing problems. Be sure, therefore, that whoever teaches you a contrary method, shows you indeed how to avoid the trouble you dread, but not how to attain the virtue you desire.

An inexperienced soldier who wants seasoning must be very discreet and cautious, suiting offensive and defensive tactics to the particular dispositions of his strength and courage; but he must never think of turning his back or quitting the fight by shunning every occasion of trouble and vexation. Such behavior may indeed remove the immediate occasion of impatience, but will leave you more vulnerable than ever to assault, for want of habitual patience.

What has been here discussed does not pertain to the vice of impurity, which, as has been observed, can only be subdued by flight.

CHAPTER THIRTY-EIGHT

THE NECESSITY OF ESTEEMING ALL OPPORTUNITIES OF FIGHTING FOR THE ACQUISITION OF VIRTUES—ESPECIALLY THOSE VIRTUES WHICH PRESENT THE GREATEST DIFFICULTIES

WE MUST NOT content ourselves with being passively receptive to opportunities of acquiring virtue; rather we must actively seek them, embracing them with alacrity when found, and delight in those opportunities that bring the most mortification as they are the most advantageous. Nothing will appear difficult to us, with the assistance of heaven, if we imprint deep in our hearts the following considerations.

The first is that opportunities actively sought are the proper, if not necessary means for acquiring virtue. Consequently, as often as we beg from God any particular virtue, we simultaneously ask for those means which He appoints for its acquisition. Otherwise our prayer would be fruitless and contradictory; it would be tempting God, Who never bestows patience but through tribulation, nor humility but through ignominy.

The same may be said of all other virtues which are the fruits of those trials God wills to send us, and which we ought to cherish in proportion to their severity, as the violence we use in disciplin-

ing ourselves is of singular efficacy in forming
habitual virtues in our souls.

Let us, therefore, be careful to mortify the will,
if only in the repression of a curious glance or
careless word. For although greater victories are
more honorable, lesser victories are more frequent.

The second consideration, to which we have already adverted, is that we may derive advantage
from all things inasmuch as they all are within
the Providence of God. Indeed, properly speaking, things, such as the sins of men, cannot be said
to happen by the wish of Him Who abhors in-
iquity; nevertheless, it is in some sense true, since
He Who has the power to prevent, permits them.

As regards our own afflictions, whether they
befall us through the fault of enemy or self, they
are, nevertheless, in God's design, however displeasing the immediate cause may be. God expects us to bear them with patience, either because
they are the means of our sanctification, or for
reasons unknown to us.

If we are convinced, then, that perfect compliance with His holy will involves patient acceptance of those evils which the malice of others
or our own sins draw upon us, how wrong, then,
must they be, who, to camouflage their own impatience, assert that an infinitely just God can
never be associated with that which proceeds from
an evil cause.

It is obvious that their only aim is to preserve
personal serenity, and persuade the world of their

privilege to reject the crosses God is pleased to send. This, however, is not all; if the thing were indifferent on other accounts, yet the delight God takes in seeing our patient acceptance of injurious treatment—particularly from those under obligation to us—would be ample justification in itself for our practice of the virtue.

The first reason is that our innate pride is more effectively curbed by the ill-usage of others, than by any voluntary, self-imposed mortifications. Secondly, in suffering patiently such situations, we conform to the requirements of God, contributing to His glory; and we attune our wills to His in circumstances in which His goodness and power are equally made manifest. Hence from so vile a thing as sin, we gather the excellent fruits of virtue and sanctity.

Know then, that God no sooner finds us resolved to attain solid virtue than He sends us trials of the severest kind. Convinced of His immense love for us and His fatherly solicitude for our spiritual advancement, we ought with gratitude to drink to the dregs of the chalice that He is pleased to offer us, confident that its beneficial character will be in proportion to its bitterness.

CHAPTER THIRTY-NINE

The Manner in Which We May Exercise the Same Virtue on Different Occasions

In a preceding chapter it was said that application to a particular virtue is preferable to embracing the practice of many at the same time; and it was said that the particular virtue upon which we have concentrated our energies must be cultivated on all occasions. Next to be presented is the manner in which this may be done with great facility.

It is possible that on the same day, perhaps in the same hour, you are reprimanded severely for some action, in itself commendable, that you are maligned in conversation, or refused in a harsh manner some small favor. Perhaps you are unjustly suspected, or employed in a disagreeable affair, or maybe your dinner is spoiled; perhaps you are overwhelmed by illness or some of the far greater evils with which this wretched existence is laden. In such a combination of vexations, there is undoubtedly opportunity for the exercise of several virtues, but according to the foregoing rule, it will be most beneficial to limit your endeavor to that virtue most desired.

If it be patience, you must strive to bear with eager courage those evils which befall you. If it be humility, you must recall in all your sufferings that they are far less than you deserve. If it be obedience, you must resign your will to the will of God Who justly punishes you.

For love of Him submit yourself, not only to rational creatures, but to situations which are the instruments of divine justice. If it be poverty, be content under your affliction, though deprived of the comforts and conveniences of life. If it be charity, exert yourself in forming acts of love of God and neighbor, remembering that when others try your patience, they present to you an opportunity of increasing your merit. And recall that God, in sending or permitting the evils which besiege you, has no other view than your spiritual good.

What has been said concerning the exercise of virtue in various situations has been an attempt to indicate a method of practicing it on a particular occasion, as in sickness or infirmity of body or mind.

CHAPTER FORTY

The Time to be Employed in the Acquisition of Each Virtue and the Indications of Our Progress

It is impossible to prescribe generally any determined space of time to be employed in the acquisition of each virtue, as this is dependent on our various states and dispositions, our progress in the devout life, and the direction of our spiritual guide. It is certain, however, that if the diligence and eagerness previously prescribed are not wanting, within a few weeks we shall make considerable progress.

A certain indication of definite advancement is perseverance in exercises of piety, in spite of all disgust, vexations, dryness, and the lack of all sensible consolation. Another no less evident mark is the incapacity of our corrupt inclinations, subdued and controlled by reason, to interrupt us in the practice of virtue. For as these inclinations decrease, virtue gains strength, and takes deeper root in our souls. Wherefore, when we feel no repugnance on the part of the inferior appetites, we may be sure that we have acquired habitual virtue; and the greater our facility in given acts, the more perfect is the habit.

You are not to imagine, however, that you have arrived at an eminent degree of sanctity, or that your passions have been entirely subdued because for a long time you have not perceived any resistance in many trials; for frequently the enemy, and our own corrupt nature, disguise themselves for a time. And thus, through a secret pride, we take that for virtue which is actually the result of vice. Moreover, if you consider the degree of perfection to which God has called you, you will perceive your previous actions to be far short of that goal. Persevere, therefore, in your exercises, as if you had just begun, never permitting the diminution of your first fervor.

Remember that it is infinitely better to advance in virtue than to be occupied in examining too closely the progress you have already made. For God, to Whom alone our hearts are known, reveals their secret to some, while He hides it from others, being mindful of particular susceptibilities to vanity or humility. Thus the Father, equally gracious and wise, takes from the weak what might occasion their ruin, and grants to the strong the means of advancing in virtue. And although unconscious of her progress, the soul must not abandon her exercises of devotion, as Almighty God will manifest that progress to her at a time when it will be most conducive to her greater welfare.

CHAPTER FORTY-ONE

THE NEED OF MODERATION IN THE DESIRE TO BE FREED OF THOSE EVILS PATIENTLY BORNE, AND THE MANNER IN WHICH OUR DESIRES ARE TO BE REGULATED

IN THE THROES of affliction of any sort, exercise patience, being oblivious of suggestions of self-love, and ignoring the tempter, who stirs up urgent desires of freedom from affliction. For from such impatience two great evils will arise. First, although you may not be entirely deprived of the habit of patience, there will remain an unfortunate disposition to impatience. The second evil is that your patience itself will be imperfect, and your recompense only proportionate to the time spent in its cultivation; whereas had you sought no relaxation, manifesting an entire resignation to the divine will, God would have rewarded for years your willingness to suffer, if the trouble itself were only of fifteen minutes duration.

Make it a general rule therefore to desire nothing but in conformity to the will of God, to form all your wishes in harmony with His; thus directed to their true end, your desires will always be just and holy, and you yourself will remain unperturbed in the joy of perfect tranquillity. For if all things are directed by Providence, to which your will is entirely comfortable, everything then will turn out according to your desires, for nothing can happen that will not be agreeable to your will.

What is here proposed does not regard the sins of ourselves or others, because sin itself is held in the utmost detestation by the Almighty; rather, our concern is with those troubles which are the punishment of offenses, or the trials of virtue, be they heart-rending sorrows or dangers to life itself. For these are the crosses with which God favors those He loves best.

Should you endeavor to mitigate your pain, and unsuccessfully employ the ordinary means to attain that end, you must resolve to bear patiently the evil you cannot remedy. You are even obliged to have recourse to such means as are commendable in themselves, and appointed by God for such ends. But let your motive for employing them be the fact that He has so ordained them, rather than attachment to self or a too eager desire of being freed from your afflictions.

CHAPTER FORTY-TWO

THE DEFENSE AGAINST THE ARTIFICES OF THE DEVIL WHEN HE SUGGESTS INDISCREET DEVOTIONS

WHEN THE DEVIL, that subtle serpent, perceives us courageously advancing towards heaven, and sees all our desires tending to God alone, fortified against ordinary satanic delusions, he transforms himself into an angel of light; he urges us to attain perfection, hurrying us on blindly and without the least regard to our own weakness.

He fills our head with devout thoughts, seconding them with passages of holy Scripture and examples drawn from the greatest saints, that he might provoke us into some shameful misstep through an indiscreet and precipitous fervor.

For example: he persuades us to chastise our bodies with excessive fasting, discipline, and similar mortifications, that, having persuaded us that we have worked wonders, he may have us fall prey to vanity, as is frequently the case in the weaker sex.

Or he hopes that we, dispirited with such penitential works as exceed our strength, may be incapable of performing any exercises of devotion; or perhaps he hopes that we, unable any longer to undergo such severities, and tiring of the practice of virtue, may return with greater fondness than ever to the vanities of the world.

Who can count the multitudes that have perished in this manner? Presumption has so blinded them that, carried away by an indiscreet zeal for suffering, they fall into the snare they themselves have helped to contrive, and they become the scorn of devils.

All of this might have been prevented had they but considered that moderation, as well as a strict regard to personal ability, must be observed in all such mortification, however commendable in themselves or however productive of excellent fruit.

For everyone is not capable of practicing the austerities of the saints, and yet every one may imitate them in many things. They may form ardent and efficacious desires of sharing in all the glorious crowns, won by the faithful soldiers of Jesus Christ in their combats; they may imitate the saints in self contempt and disdain for the world, in their silence and retirement, in their humility and charity to all men, in their patient endurance of the greatest injuries, in rendering good for the evil of their worst enemies, and in their care to avoid the smallest faults. All of these things are infinitely more meritorious in the sight of God, than all the corporal severities we could possibly exercise.

It must be similarly observed that at first it is advisable to use moderation in external penances, for it is better that we have room to increase them if necessary, rather than endanger our capacity for performing any by imprudent zeal. I mention this because I am willing to believe that you do not succumb to the gross error of making an idol of your health. This type is ever in dread of the least irregularity, and its entire study and conversation is devoted to the means of avoiding sickness. Extremely fastidious as regards eating, such people, rather than strengthening, often ruin their stomachs by the constant use of choice foods, and yet they would have the world believe that they have no other view than the preservation of themselves for the glory of God.

Thus do they cloak their sensuality, while their actual design is the union of two irreconcilable enemies, the flesh and the spirit. Such an attitude inevitably results in ruin of both health and devotion, both of which suffer in this delusion. Consequently, those who make the greatest and surest advances in devotion are those who live in a plain, unpretentious manner.

In all things, however, discretion must be used, and due regard had for the exigencies of different constitutions which are not all similarly fitted for the same exercises. This is to be understood, not only of exterior mortifications, but even of mental disciplines, as has been discussed previously in treating of the method of gradual acquisition of the loftiest virtues.

CHAPTER FORTY-THREE

The Tendency of Our Corrupt Natures, Prompted By the Devil, to Indulge in Rash Judgment, and the Remedy for This Evil

SMUG SELF-SATISFACTION is responsible for another great disorder, which is rash judgment. This vice, which we not only encourage in ourselves, but infuse into others, springs from and is nourished by pride; and in proportion to our acceptance of it is our growing conceit and danger of further delusions by the devil. For by degrees we assume for ourselves what we detract from others, foolishly imagining ourselves exempt from the sins for which we so readily condemn our neighbors.

The enemy of our souls no sooner discovers this malicious tendency, but he immediately employs all his artifices to make us attentive to the failings of others, and magnify those failings out of all proportion. He goes to ineffable depths in making us aware of our neighbor's most trivial peccadillo, in the absence of a more glaring fault.

Since, therefore, he is so viciously clever and intent upon our ruin, we must be no less vigilant in discovering and defeating his designs. When he suggests the sins of others to us, we must banish all such thoughts, and if he persists in tricking us into rash judgments, we are to cultivate a deep abhorrence for such malicious insinuations. Let us remember that we are not ordinarily authorized to judge others, but if we are, how seldom equity guides us, blinded as we are by prejudice and passion, and inclined to impute the worst of motives to others in their thoughts and actions.

The most efficacious remedy of this evil is a constant awareness of our own wretchedness, for when we find so much room for improvement in ourselves we have little inclination to judge and condemn others. Moreover, in sedulously seeking out our own shortcomings, we shall free our minds from a certain malignity which is the source of rash judgment. For whoever unjustly condemns his neighbor has good reason for suspecting himself guilty of the same crime, inasmuch as vicious men are prone to think others like themselves.

When, therefore, we find ourselves inclined to condemn others, let us inwardly accuse ourselves with this just reproof: "Blind and presumptuous wretch, how dare you rashly examine your neighbor's actions—you who have the same if not greater sins to answer for?" Thus in turning these weapons against ourselves, what might have been injurious to our neighbor becomes beneficial to us.

Even if a neighbor's fault be publicly known, let charity suggest some excuse. Let us believe there are some hidden virtues, for the preservation of which God is pleased to permit the publicized deficiency; and let us hope that the fault in which God suffers him to remain for a time, may eventually bring the erring one to true self-knowledge, that being despised by others, he may learn the lesson of humility. Such a defeat is really a victory.

Where the sin, besides being commonly known, is also of the utmost gravity, and the sinner hardened in impenitence, we should raise our hearts to heaven in deference to the inscrutable wisdom of God. For we should be mindful that many have emerged from the depths of depravity to become saints, while others have fallen from angelic heights of perfection to satanic depths of sinfulness.

These reflections should convince every thinking person that carping criticism should begin with oneself. If one finds himself favorably disposed toward his neighbor, it is owing to the inspiration of the Holy Spirit, whereas his rash judgments, dislike and contempt of others, owe their rise to his own malice and the promptings of the devil.

Let us remember then that, if ever we find ourselves too attentive to the failings of others, we must not cease until we have entirely erased them from memory.

CHAPTER FORTY-FOUR

PRAYER

WE HAVE SHOWN that distrustfulness of self, confidence in God, and proper application of the faculties of the soul are the indispensable weapons of conquest in the spiritual combat. Yet a far more important weapon is prayer, since by it are obtained, not only the above-specified virtues, but everything requisite for our salvation. Prayer is the channel of all divine grace; by it God is compelled, as it were, to grant us the strength of heaven, and destroy by our weak hands the fiercest of our foes. But in order to receive full benefit from our prayer, the following method should be observed:

1. We must desire sincerely to serve God with ardent fervor in the manner most agreeable to Him; and this desire will be enkindled within our breasts if we consider three things attentively. The first is that Almighty God deserves our homage and service by reason of the excellence of His sovereign being, His goodness, beauty, wisdom, power, and His ineffable, infinite perfection. The second is that God in heaven became man on earth to consecrate a life of thirty-three years to the cause of our salvation. He condescended to dress our wounds with His own hands, and heal them, not with oil and wine, but with His own

precious blood and immaculate body, torn and disfigured by cruel whips, thorns, and nails. The third point is our realization of the obligation to observe His law, and discharge every duty, since this is the only way we can expect to triumph over the devil, to become masters of ourselves, and children of God.

2. We must have a vibrant, living faith and a firm confidence that God will not refuse the assistance necessary to serve Him faithfully and work out our salvation. A soul rekindled with this holy confidence is like a sacred vessel, into which divine Mercy pours the treasures of His grace; and the larger the vessel, the greater the abundance of heavenly blessings it receives through prayer. For how can God, Whose power is limitless, and Whose goodness is alien to all deception, ever refuse His gifts to those whose petitions He has encouraged, and whose perseverance and faith He has promised to reward with the blessings of the Holy Spirit?

3. But our motive for prayer must be the will of God rather than the will of self. We must apply ourselves to this divinely appointed duty because He has commanded it, and we must wish no more than that which is in utter conformity to God's plan. Thus, our intention will not be to make the divine will subservient to our own, but rather to transform the human will so that it is in complete harmony with the divine.

The reason for this humble accedence to the divine will is the perversity of our own, tainted as it is with a blind self-love. Guided by ourselves alone, we would err and stumble, but the will of God, essentially just and holy, cannot be mistaken. Thus the will of God should be the will of men, since not to follow the former is to go astray. Let us, then, be most solicitous that all our petitions be agreeable to God, and if doubts arise concerning the concurrence of the human with the divine, let a humble submission to divine Providence accompany our requests. If, however, the things we ask are, by their very nature, pleasing to Him, such as grace, virtue, etc., then let us beg them with a view to pleasing and serving His divine Majesty, rather than for any other consideration, however creditable.

4. If we wish our prayers to be efficacious, our actions must suit the petitions, and we must exert much energy in making ourselves worthy of the favors we ask. For prayer and interior mortification are inseparable, and he that seeks a particular virtue, without making a serious effort to practice it, only tempts God.

5. Before we ask anything of God, we ought to thank Him most humbly for the innumerable benefits He has graciously bestowed upon us. Let us say to Him: "O Lord, Who after creating me, didst mercifully pay the price of my redemption, delivering me from the fury of myriad enemies, come now to my assistance; and forgetting my past ingratitude, bestow upon me this favor I now ask."

If, however, at the very time we seek to attain a particular virtue, we find ourselves tempted to the contrary vice, let us thank God for granting us the opportunity of practicing the virtue in question, and look upon the occasion as a favor.

6. As the entire force and efficacy of prayer is attributed solely to the goodness of God, at the conclusion of our petitions we should constantly remember the merits of our Saviour's life and passion, and His promise to graciously hear our requests, with one or the other of these sentences:

a) "I beseech Thee, O Lord, through Thy infinite mercy, to grant my petition."

b) "Through the merits of Thy Son, bestow this favor on me."

c) "Be mindful, O God, of Thy promises, and hear my prayers."

Again, we may have recourse to the intercession of the blessed Mother and the other saints; for they prevail much with God, Who is pleased to honor them, in proportion to the honor they accorded Him on earth.

7. We must persist in prayer, since God certainly cannot overlook our humble perseverance. For if the pleadings of the widow in the Gospel prevailed with the wicked judge, how can our pleadings be ignored by God, Who is infinitely good? Thus, although our favors may not be immediately granted, and may even appear to be ignored by God, we must not lose our confidence in His infinite goodness, nor desist from prayer. For God possesses both immense power and will to grant us those things conducive to our ultimate

welfare. Therefore, if we are not wanting in ourselves, we shall inevitably obtain what we ask for, something better, or perhaps both. As for the rest, the more we churlishly think ourselves slighted by God, the more we should hold ourselves in contempt. But in considering our misery, we should contemplate the divine mercy, and far from lessening our confidence in Him, we must increase it; for the steadier we remain in situations attended by fear and diffidence, the greater will be our merit.

Finally, let us never cease to thank God, blessing equally His wisdom, His goodness, His charity, whether He grants or refuses our petition. Whatever happens, let us be undisturbed, contented and resigned to divine Providence in all things.

CHAPTER FORTY-FIVE

MENTAL PRAYER

MENTAL PRAYER is the elevation of our minds to God, asking of Him either expressly or tacitly those things of which we stand in need. We ask for them expressly when we say in our hearts: "O my God, grant me this request for the honor of Thy holy name"; or "Lord, I am firmly convinced that this petition is Thy will, and for Thy greater honor, I ask this petition. Accomplish, therefore, Thy divine will in me."

When harassed by the attacks of the enemy, let us say: "Come swiftly, O Lord, to my assistance lest I fall a prey to my enemy"; or "O God, my refuge and my strength, help me speedily, lest I perish." When temptation continues, we must continue the same prayer, courageously resisting the foe; and when the fury of the combat has passed, let us address ourselves to the Almighty, imploring Him to consider our weakness in the face of the enemy's strength: "Behold, my God, Thy creature, the work of Thy hands, a man redeemed by Thy precious blood. And behold Satan trying to carry him from Thee to utterly destroy him. It is to Thee I fly for aid, and it is in Thee that I place my entire confidence, for I know that Thou alone art infinitely good and powerful. Have pity on a miserable creature who stumbles

blindly, though willfully, into the path of his enemies, as do all who forsake the assistance of Thy
grace. Help me therefore, my only hope, O sole
strength of my soul!"

We tacitly ask favors of God when we present
to Him our necessities, without making any particular request. Placing ourselves in His divine
presence, we acknowledge our incapacity to avoid
evil or do good without His aid. We are nevertheless inflamed with a desire of serving Him. Thus
we must fix our eyes upon Him, waiting for His
assistance with unbounded confidence and utter
humility.

The confession of our weakness and the desire
to serve Him, this act of faith so performed, is a
silent prayer which will infallibly obtain our request from heaven. The more sincere the confession, the more ardent the desire, and the more
lively the faith, the greater will be the efficacy of
the prayer before the throne of God.

There is another method of prayer similar to
this, but more concise, consisting as it does in but
a single act of the soul. The soul presents her requests to the Almighty, adverting to a favor already asked and still sought, although not
formally expressed.

Let us endeavor to cultivate this kind of prayer,
and employ it on all occasions; for experience will
convince us that nothing is more easy, yet nothing
more excellent and efficacious.

CHAPTER FORTY-SIX

MEDITATION

WHEN A CONSIDERABLE length of time (as a half-hour, hour, or an even longer period) is to be spent in prayer, it is advisable to make a meditation on some feature of our Saviour's life or passion; the reflections naturally arising from such meditation should then be applied to the particular virtue we are striving to attain.

If, for instance, you need patience, contemplate the mystery of your Saviour scourged at the pillar. Consider first the blows and revilements hurled at Him by the soldiers as they brutally drag their innocent victim to the appointed place as ordered. Secondly, consider Him stripped of His garments, exposed to the piercing cold. Thirdly, picture those innocent hands, bound tightly to the pillar. Fourthly, consider His body, torn with whips until His blood moistened the earth. And finally, envision the frequency of the blows, creating new wounds, reopening others on that sacred body.

Dwelling on these or similar details, calculated to inspire in you a love of patience, you should try to feel within your very soul the inexpressible anguish so patiently borne by your divine Master. Then consider the excruciating agony of His spirit, and the patience and mildness with which that agony was endured by Him Who was ready to suffer even more for God's glory and your welfare.

Behold, then, your Master, covered with blood, desiring nothing more earnestly than your patient acceptance of affliction; and be assured that He implores for you the assistance of the Heavenly Father that you may bear with resignation, not only the cross of the moment, but the crosses to come. Strengthen, therefore, by frequent acts your resolution to suffer with joy; and, raising your mind to heaven, give thanks to the Father of mercies, Who didst send His only Son into this world to suffer indescribable torments, and to intercede for you in your necessities.

Conclude your meditation by beseeching Him to grant you the virtue of patience, through the merits and intercession of this beloved Son in Whom He is well pleased.

CHAPTER FORTY-SEVEN

ANOTHER METHOD OF MEDITATION

THERE IS ANOTHER method of prayer and meditation besides the one to which we have adverted. In this latter method, having considered the poignant sufferings of your Saviour and His patient endurance of them, you proceed to two other considerations of equal importance.

The one is the consideration of Christ's infinite merits, and the other, of that satisfaction and glory which the eternal Father received from His obedience—an obedience unto death, even the death of the Cross.

You must represent these two considerations to the divine Majesty, as two powerful means of obtaining the grace you seek. This method is applicable, not only to all the mysteries of Our Lord's passion, but to every exterior or interior act He performed in the course of His passion.

CHAPTER FORTY-EIGHT

A Method of Prayer Based On the Intercession of the Blessed Virgin

Besides the methods of meditation already mentioned, there is another which is addressed particularly to the Blessed Virgin. We first consider the eternal Father, then Jesus Christ Our Lord, and finally, the Blessed Mother.

With regard to the eternal Father, there are two considerations. The first is the singular affection He cherished from all eternity for this most chaste Virgin whom He chose to be the mother of His divine Son. The second is the eminent sanctity He was pleased to bestow upon her and the many virtues she practiced in her lifetime.

Meditating on the affection of the eternal Father for our Lady, you must begin by raising your mind above all created beings; look forward to the vast expanses of eternity, enter into the heart of God, and see with what delight He viewed the person destined one day to become the mother of His Son; beseech Him by that delight to give you sufficient strength against your enemies, especially those who most grievously afflict you. Contemplate, then, the virtues and heroic actions of this incomparable Virgin; make an offering of each or all of them to God, as they are of such efficacy as to obtain for you divine assistance in your particular necessities.

After this address yourself to Jesus, begging Him to be mindful of that loving mother who for nine months carried Him in her womb, and from the moment of His birth paid Him the most profound adoration. For this was her acknowledgment that this Child was at once God and man, her Creator and her Son. With compassion she saw Him poorly accommodated in a humble stable, nourished Him with her pure milk, kissed and embraced Him a thousand times with maternal fondness, and through His life and at His death, suffered for Him beyond expression. Present this picture to the Saviour, that He may be compelled, as it were, by such powerful motives, to hear your prayers.

Appeal to the Blessed Virgin herself, reminding her of her commission from all eternity, to be the Mother of Mercy and the refuge of sinners, and that after her divine Son, you place your greatest confidence in her intercession. Present to her the fact, asserted by the learned and confirmed by miracles, that no one ever called upon her with a lively faith, and was left unaided.

Finally, remind her of the sufferings of her Son for your salvation, that she may obtain of Him the grace necessary to make proper use of His sufferings for the greater glory of that loving Saviour.

CHAPTER FORTY-NINE

SOME CONSIDERATIONS TO INDUCE CONFIDENCE IN THE ASSISTANCE OF THE BLESSED VIRGIN

WHOEVER WISHES to have recourse to the Blessed Virgin confidently must observe the following motives.

1. Experience teaches us that a vessel which has contained perfumes preserves their odor, especially if the perfume is in the container for any length of time, or if any remain in it; yet here there is but a limited power, similar to the warmth carried from a fire, the source of that warmth.

If such be the case, what are we to say of the charity and compassion of the Blessed Virgin, who for nine months bore, and still carries in her heart, the only Son of God, the uncreated charity which knows no bounds? If, as often as we approach a fire, we are affected by its heat, have we not reason to believe that whoever approaches the heart of the Mother of Mercies, ever burning with her most ardent charity, must be profoundly affected in proportion to the frequency of his petitions, the humility and confidence in his heart?

2. No creature ever loved Jesus Christ more ardently, nor showed more perfect submission to His will, than Mary, His mother. If then, this Saviour, immolated for us sinners, gave His

mother to us, an advocate and intercessor for all
time, she cannot but comply with His request, and
will not refuse us her assistance. Let us, then, not
hesitate to implore her pity; let us have recourse
to her with great confidence in all our necessities,
as she is an inexhaustible source of blessings, bestowing her favors in proportion to the confidence
placed in her.

CHAPTER FIFTY

A Method of Meditation and Prayer Involving the Intercession of the Saints and the Angels

THE TWO FOLLOWING METHODS of obtaining the protection of the saints and angels may be employed.

The first method is to address yourself to the eternal Father, laying before Him the hymns of heavenly choirs, the labors, persecutions, and torments suffered by the saints on earth for love of Him. Then, in recalling their fidelity and love, beseech Him to grant your petitions.

The second method is to invoke the angels, those blessed spirits earnestly desirous, not only of our earthly perfection, but of our greater heavenly perfection. Earnestly beseech them to assist you in subduing your evil inclinations and conquering the enemies of your salvation; and beg a particular remembrance at the hour of death.

Sometimes think over the extraordinary graces God has granted to the saints and angels, and rejoice as if they had been bestowed on yourself. Rather, let your joy be even greater for His having bestowed such favors on them rather than on yourself, for such was His will; and you should bless and praise God in the accomplishment of His divine plan.

To facilitate the regularity and performance of this exercise, it would be well to assign the different days of the week to the different orders of the blessed. On Sunday, implore the intercession of the nine angelic choirs; on Monday, invoke John the Baptist; on Tuesday, the patriarchs and prophets; on Wednesday, the apostles; on Thursday, the martyrs; on Friday, bishops and confessors; on Saturday, the virgins and other saints. But let no day pass without imploring the assistance of Our Lady, the queen of all the saints, your guardian angel, the glorious archangel St. Michael, or any other saint to whom you have any particular devotion.

Moreover, beseech daily the eternal Father, His divine Son, and the Blessed Virgin, that you may be particularly under the protection of St. Joseph, the worthy spouse of the most chaste of virgins. Then addressing yourself to this loving protector, ask with great humility to be received into his care. For innumerable are the instances of assistance afforded to those who have called upon St. Joseph in their spiritual or temporal necessities. Particularly has he aided them when they stood in need of light from heaven, and direction in their prayers. And if God shows so much regard for the other saints who have loved and served Him here below, how much consideration and deference will He not show for the person He so honored as to pay him filial homage and obedience?

CHAPTER FIFTY-ONE

Meditation on the Sufferings of Christ and the Sentiments to be Derived from Contemplation of Them

What I prescribed previously concerning the method of praying and meditating on the sufferings of our Lord and Saviour regarded only the petition of those things of which we stand in need; now we are to proceed to the adoption of the proper sentiments from our considerations. For instance, if you have chosen the crucifixion and its attendant circumstances as the subject of your meditation, you may dwell on the following considerations.

Consider first the arrival of Jesus on Mount Calvary. His executioners rudely stripped Him, tearing off the garments which adhered to the torn flesh of His lacerated body. Consider next the fresh wounds made in His Sacred Head by the crown of thorns, removed and reset by his barbarous executioners. Next, visualize Him nailed to the cross with spikes, driven through the flesh and wood with a large hammer. Consider that His hands, not reaching the places designed for them, were stretched so violently that all His bones were disjointed, enabling the onlooker to count His very bones (Psalm XXL, 18). Then think of the actual elevation of the cross, and the weight of Christ's body resting on nails which tore gaping wounds in His hands and feet, giving Him excruciating pain.

If, by these and similar considerations you wish to enkindle the flames of divine love within your heart, try to attain by meditation a sublime knowledge of the infinite goodness of your Saviour, Who for you condescended to suffer so much. For the more you advance in the knowledge of His love for you, the greater will be your love and affection for Him. Being convinced of His extraordinary charity, you will naturally conceive a sincere sorrow for having so often and so heinously offended Him, Who offered Himself as a sacrifice for your offenses.

Proceed then to make acts of hope, considering that this great God on the cross had no other plan than to extirpate sin from the world, to free you from the devil, to expiate your crimes, to reconcile you to His Father, and to provide a resource for you in all your necessities. But if, after contemplating His passion, you consider its effects, your sorrow will be turned into joy. For observe that by Christ's death the sins of humanity were blotted out, the anger of a sovereign Judge appeased, the powers of hell defeated, death itself vanquished, and the places of the fallen angels filled in heaven. And the joy arising from such reflection will be increased by thinking of the joy with which the Holy Trinity, the Blessed Virgin, the church militant and triumphant received the glad tidings of the redemption of mankind.

If you would have a lively sorrow for your sins,

let your meditation convince you that if Jesus Christ suffered so much, it was to inspire you with wholesome self-contempt, and a hatred of your disorderly passions, particularly your greatest faults, which are naturally most offensive to Almighty God.

And if you would excite sentiments of admiration, you need only consider that nothing is more shocking than the sight of the Creator of the universe, the fountain of life, butchered by His own creatures, the right of the supreme majesty, as it were, annihilated, justice condemned, beauty defiled and lost in filth, the beloved of the Eternal Father become the hated of sinners. Light inaccessible is overwhelmed by the powers of darkness; uncreated glory and felicity are buried under ignominy and wretchedness.

To arouse compassion in your heart for the sufferings of your Saviour and God, exclusive of His exterior pains, consider the most acute of His sufferings, His interior anguish. For if you are moved by the first, you will be pierced with grief at the sight of the second. The soul of Christ beheld the divinity then as clearly as it does now in heaven. It knew how much God deserved to be honored, and as it infinitely loved Him, desired that all creatures should love Him with all the power of their souls. Seeing Him, therefore, so horribly dishonored throughout the world by countless, abominable crimes, it was overwhelmed with grief that the divine majesty was not loved and served by all men. As the greatness of this desire of the soul of Christ that His Father be loved was beyond imagination, it is futile to try to comprehend the depths of His interior sufferings in the agonies of death.

Moreover, as this divine Saviour loved mankind to an ineffable degree, such an ardent and tender love must have caused Him much sorrow for the sins that would tear men from Him. For He knew that no one could sin mortally without destroying that sanctifying grace which is the bond between Him and the just. And this separation would cause Jesus greater anguish of soul than dislocated limbs caused His body. For the soul, altogether spiritual and immeasurably superior to the body, is much more delicately attuned to pain. But of all the afflictions of our blessed Saviour, the most grievous, doubtless, was the sight of the damned, incapable of repentance, who must inevitably be banished from Him for all eternity.

If the contemplation of such suffering moves you to compassion for your dying Jesus, meditate further, and you will find that His excessive suffering was not caused by your sins alone; for His precious blood was shed not only to cleanse you from the sins you have committed, but to preserve you from those you might have committed were you unaided by heaven. It is a fact that you will never be without motives for taking part in the sufferings of Jesus crucified. Know, moreover, that human nature never was, and never will be subject to any affliction that was unknown to Him. He suffered from injuries, reproaches, temptations, pains, loss of goods, voluntary austerities more acutely than those who groan under them. For as this tender Saviour had a perfect comprehension of any affliction of mind or body to which we are prone—even to the least pain or headache—He must certainly have been moved with great compassion for us.

Who, however, can express what He felt at the sight of His Blessed Mother's affliction? For she shared in all the pangs and outrages which attended His passion, and with the same views and from the same motives. And although her sufferings were infinitely short of His, they were excruciating beyond expression. The awareness of our Lady's agony redoubled the sorrows of Jesus, and pierced His heart still deeper. Hence it was that a certain devout soul compared the heart of Jesus to a burning furnace in which He voluntarily suffered from the ardent flames of divine love.

And after all, what is the cause of such unspeakable agony? Nothing but our sins; this is the answer. Therefore, the greatest compassion and gratitude we can possibly show towards Him Who has suffered so much for us, is to be truly sorry for our past offenses out of pure love for Him; to detest sin with all the fervor of our soul because it is displeasing to Him; and to wage ceaseless war against our evil inclinations because they are His greatest enemies. Thus divesting ourselves of the old man, and putting on the new, we adorn our souls with virtue, in which alone their beauty consists.

CHAPTER FIFTY-TWO

THE BENEFITS DERIVED FROM MEDITATIONS ON THE CROSS, AND THE IMITATION OF THE VIRTUE OF CHRIST CRUCIFIED

GREAT ARE THE ADVANTAGES to be derived from meditating on the cross, the first of which is, not only a detestation of past sins, but also the firm resolution to fight against our ever present disorderly appetites, which crucified our Saviour. The second advantage is the forgiveness of sins, obtained from Jesus crucified, and a wholesome self-contempt which inspires us forever to forsake offending Him, and continually to love and serve Him with all our hearts in acknowledgment of what He suffered for our sakes. The third is the unceasing labor with which we root out all depraved habits, however trivial they may appear. The fourth consists in our ardent efforts to imitate our divine Master, Who died, not only to expiate our sins, but to bequeath to us the sublime example of a life of sanctity and perfection.

The following method of meditation will be highly serviceable, assuming as I do, that you particularly wish to imitate the patience of your Saviour in carrying your crosses. Consider well these several points:

1. What the soul of Christ suffered for God.
2. What God did for the soul of Jesus.

3. What the soul of Jesus did for itself and its body.

4. What Jesus did for us.

5. What we ought to do for Jesus.

1. Consider in the first place, that the soul of Jesus engulfed in the ocean of divinity, contemplated that infinite and incomprehensible Being, before Whom even the most exalted of creatures is utterly insignificant; contemplated, I say, in a state so debased as to suffer the vilest indignities of ungrateful man, without the least diminution of its essential glory and splendor. And from the depths of its suffering, the soul of Christ adored its sovereign Majesty, giving it myriad thanks and accepting all for its sake.

2. Behold on the other hand what God bestowed on the soul of Jesus; consider that the divine will decreed the scourgings, spittle, blasphemies, buffetings, crown of thorns for love of us, and the crucifixion, which were meted out to Jesus, the only and beloved Son of God. See with what delight God, knowing the admirable end to which it was all directed, beheld His divine Son, loaded with infamy and overwhelmed with affliction.

3. Contemplate next the soul of Jesus, and observe with what alacrity it submitted itself to the will of God, either because of the immensity of its divine perfection, or the infinity of divine favor bestowed upon it. Who can describe the ardent affection of this soul for crosses? This was a soul that sought even new ways of suffering, and fail-

ing in this, abandoned itself and the innocent body to the mercy of miscreants and the powers of hell.

4. Turn, then, your eyes to Jesus, Who from the midst of His agony, addresses you in this affectionate manner: "See to what depths of misery I am reduced by thy ungovernable will, which refuses the least constraint in compliance with mine. Behold the horrible pains I endure, with no other purpose than to teach thee a lesson of patience. And let me persuade thee, by all these sufferings, to accept with resignation this cross I here present, and those which I shall send in the future. Surrender thy reputation to calumny, and thy body to the fury of the persecutors whom I shall choose for thy trial, however vile and inhuman they may be. Oh, that thou didst know what delight thy patience and resignation afford me! But then, how canst thou be ignorant of it, when thou beholdest these wounds received to purchase for thee those virtues with which I would adorn thy soul, more dear to me than life itself? If I have suffered this debasement for thee, canst thou not bear a light affliction, in order to lessen My agony to some degree? Canst thou refuse to heal those wounds I have received through thy impatience, wounds more cruel to me than physical anguish?"

5. Consider who it is that speaks thus to you; consider that it is Jesus Christ, the King of Glory, true God and true Man. Consider too the magnitude of His torments and humiliations, greater than that deserved by the most vicious of crim-

inals. Be astonished to behold Him in the midst
of these agonies, not only firm and resolute, but
even replenished with joy, as if the day of His
passion was a day of triumph. Just as a few drops
of water sprinkled upon a flame only adds a fresh
intensity to its glow, so did His torments, embraced in a charity which made the burden seem
light, serve to augment his joy and desire of suffering still greater affliction.

Moreover, reflect that throughout His entire
life, He was motivated, not by compulsion or self-
interest, but rather by pure love alone, that you
may learn from Him the manner of practicing patience. Endeavor, therefore, to attain a perfect
knowledge of what He demands of you, and consider His delight at your practice of patience.
Then form an ardent desire of carrying this cross
and heavier ones, not only with patience, but with
joy, that you may more exactly imitate Christ crucified and render yourself more acceptable to Him.

Picture to ourself all the torments and indignities of His passion, and amazed at His constancy,
blush at your own weakness. Look upon your
sufferings as merely imaginative when compared
to His, and regard your patience as not even the
faintest adumbration of His. Dread nothing so
much as an unwillingness to suffer for your
Saviour, rejecting such unwillingness as a suggestion from hell.

Consider Jesus on the cross as you would a devout book worthy of your unceasing study and by
which you may learn the practice of the most he-

roic virtues. This is the book which may be truly called the "Book of Life" (Apocalypse, III, 5), which at once enlightens the mind by its doctrines and inflames the will by its examples. The world is full of books, but were it possible for man to read them all, he would never be so well instructed to hate vice and embrace virtue as by contemplating a crucified God. But remember that there are those who spend hours lamenting the passion of our Lord and admiring His patience, and yet on the first occasion betray as great an impatience in suffering as if they had never thought of the cross. Such men are like untried soldiers, who in their barracks breathe nothing but conquest, but on the first appearance of the enemy, beat a hasty and inglorious retreat. What is more despicable after considering, admiring and extolling the virtues of our Redeemer, than to forget them all in an instant when an opportunity of practicing them presents itself?

CHAPTER FIFTY-THREE

CONCERNING THE MOST HOLY SACRAMENT
OF THE EUCHARIST

THUS FAR, I have tried, as perhaps you have observed, to furnish you with four kinds of spiritual weapons, and the methods by which they may be profitably employed; it remains to present to you the invaluable aids to be derived from the Holy Eucharist in subduing the enemies of perfection and salvation. As this sublime sacrament towers above the others in dignity and efficacy, it is the most terrible of all weapons to the infernal powers.

The methods previously treated have no force but through the merits of Jesus Christ, and by the grace He has purchased for us by His precious blood; but the Eucharist is Jesus Christ Himself, His body, His blood, His soul and divinity. The former methods are bestowed upon us by God that we may use them in subduing the enemy through Jesus Christ; but the Eucharist is given that we may fight against the enemy with Him. For by eating the body of Jesus, and drinking His blood we dwell in Him and He in us. We may eat His body and drink His blood in reality every day, and spiritually every hour, both of which are highly profitable and holy. The latter should be practiced as often as possible, the former as often as shall be judged expedient.

CHAPTER FIFTY-FOUR

The Manner in Which We Ought to Receive the Blessed Sacrament

THE MOTIVES for approaching this divine sacrament are many, from which it follows that there are various requirements to be observed at three different times:

1. Before Communion
2. At the moment of reception of Communion
3. After Communion

1. Before Communion, whatever be our motive, we must, if stained with mortal sin, cleanse ourselves in the sacrament of Penance. And with all sincerity of heart, we must offer ourselves to Jesus Christ, consecrating our souls and all their faculties to His service. For it is in this sacrament that He bestows to mankind His body, blood, soul, and divinity, together with the immense and inexhaustible treasure of His infinite merits. And as all of our gifts to Him are insignificant when compared to His gifts to us, we should desire nothing less than the totality of merits gained by the created beings of the universe to offer as a present deserving His regard.

If our desire is victory over spiritual adversaries, we should meditate for some time previous to the reception of Communion on the incomprehensibly ardent desire of our Saviour to be one with us in suppressing our inordinate appetites.

In order, however, to formulate some idea of this divine wish in our regard, we might consider two things. The first is the ineffable joy with which wisdom incarnate dwells among us, for He calls it His delight (Prov. VIII, 31). The second is the implacable hatred He bears toward mortal sin, inasmuch as it is both an insuperable obstacle to that much-desired intimate union with Him, and in utter opposition to His divine perfections. For as God is sovereignly good, a light undimmed and beauty inviolate, He must inevitably hate sin which is all malice, all darkness, and all corruption. So burning indeed is this hatred of God for sin, that the entire dispensation of the Old and New Testaments has been ordained for its destruction. Several of God's saints have said that divinity would have suffered a thousand deaths on a thousand Golgothas if the smallest faults could be annihilated within us.

These considerations, rudimentary as they are, may enable you to see how much our Saviour desires to dwell within our hearts to expiate therefrom our common enemies; thus we should welcome Him with all the fervor of which we are capable. The joyful expectancy of His arrival will raise our courage, and inspire us to war anew on our predominant passion by performing many acts of the contrary virtue. Particularly should this be so on the evening before and on the morning of our reception of Holy Communion.

2. When we are about to receive the body of Our Lord, let us quickly consider the faults com-

mitted since our last communion, and in order to conceive a more perfect sorrow, let us remember that we committed them as callously as if Christ had not died for us on Calvary's tree. Such a remembrance should fill us with shame and fear for having basely preferred a trifling compliance to our own will to the obedience due so gracious a master. But when we consider that in spite of this ingratitude and infidelity, this God of all charity still condescends to visit us and live within us, then let us approach Him with confidence and open hearts; for when He lives within, no tainted affections of the world may steal in.

3. After Communion, we are to remain in profound recollection, adoring Our Lord with great humility and saying within our souls: "Thou seest, O God of my soul, my wretched propensity to sin; Thou seest how domineering is this passion, and that of myself I cannot resist. It is Thou Who must fight my battles, and if I share in the combat, it is Thee from Whom I must expect the crown of victory!"

Then addressing ourselves to the Eternal Father, let us offer to Him this beloved Son Who now dwells within our breast; let us offer Him thanks for innumerable benefits and implore Him for the grace that will make our victory complete.

Finally, let us resolve to fight courageously against the enemy from whom we suffer most. Thus we may expect victory, since if we are not wanting in petition, God is not wanting in bestowing, and sooner or later victory will be ours.

CHAPTER FIFTY-FIVE

PREPARATION FOR COMMUNION, AND THE ROLE OF THE EUCHARIST IN EXCITING IN US A LOVE OF GOD

IF OUR MOTIVE in receiving Holy Communion be a desire of increasing our love of God, we should recall the love which God has for us. The preparation consists in an attentive contemplation of this Sovereign Lord of boundless power and majesty, Who not satisfied with creating us to His image and likeness, nor with the immolation of His only Son in our behalf, left this Son to us in the sacrament of the Eucharist to be our food and support in all our necessities. Consider well the greatness and uniqueness of this love in the following manner:

1. In its duration we find that God's love for us is eternal and unceasing; for as He is eternal in His divinity, so is He eternal in His love. Before time was, God determined to give His Son to mankind in this marvellous manner. Let these words, then, echo joyfully within your heart: "In the abyss of eternity, my littleness was so loved by the most high God, that He thought of me, and with love ineffable wished to give me His Son to be my food and my nourishment!"

2. Our strongest passions for earthly things recognize certain limits which they cannot exceed,

but the love of God for us is limitless. The advent of His Son, equal to Him in majesty and perfection, was a testimony to that boundless love. Thus is the gift equal to the love, and the love to the gift; and both are infinite, beyond the borders of human understanding.

3. In loving us God was not constrained by any power or necessity, but heaped innumerable benefits upon us out of the magnitude of divine love.

4. Neither have human merit or previous good works rendered us worthy of this remarkable gift. If God has loved to excess or given of Himself unstintingly, it is rather to be attributed to the immensity of divine charity.

5. God's love for us is untainted with the blemish of the self-interest present in human affections. For what is the totality of human greatness to Him, the source of all happiness and glory? How could we possibly add glory to glory itself? The advantages, then, are all on the side of man.

Meditating on this truth, let each man say within himself: "Who could have imagined, O Lord, that a God of such infinite greatness would bestow His affections on such an abject and insignificant creature as myself! What could be Thy design, O King of glory? What canst Thou expect of me who am but dust? I see clearly, O my God, by the light of Thy burning charity which enlightens me with knowledge and enkindles me with love, that Thy design was one divorced from all self-interest. For Thy wish in so graciously bestowing this sacrament is to transform me into

Thee, that I may live in Thee and Thou in me. Such an intimate union will ultimately remake my heart, fashioning from a vessel of earth, a delicate instrument attuned to things divine."

Then, full of joy and wonder at the indications of divine love given us by Christ, and aware that His only purpose is the transformation of our hearts from things of earth to things of heaven, let us offer a sacrifice, and consecrate the will, the memory, and understanding to the sole task of pleasing Him in the gracious acceptance of His holy will.

After this, recognizing our incapacity to dispose ourselves properly, unaided by His grace for proper reception of the Eucharist, let us strive earnestly to obtain that grace by ejaculations such as the following:

"O heavenly food, when shall I be united to Thee, to be consumed joyfully in the fire of divine love? O divine charity, when shall I live in Thee, by Thee, and for Thee alone? O heavenly manna, sovereign good, joy of my heart, when shall I, loathing all other food, seek Thee alone? O life of eternal joy, when shall I dwell in Thee alone? O my loving and almighty Lord, free my heart from the tyranny of its passions and vicious attachments; adorn it with Thy heavenly virtues, and with gentle compulsion force it to rejoice in loving and pleasing Thee. Then O Lord, will I open my heart and bid Thee enter; then shalt Thou come, my only treasure, to transform my heart by Thy divine presence."

Such are the tender and affectionate sentiments which we should form on the evening before, and on the morning of reception of Holy Communion.

When the time itself draws near, we must consider attentively who it is that we are about to receive; for our guest is to be the Son of the living God, the august majesty before Whom the heavens and the powers of heaven tremble in awesome fear. Our guest is to be the saint of saints, mirror without blemish, purity itself, before Whom all is unclean in comparison. This is divinity become man; one looked upon as the very outcast of men, Who was pleased to be spat upon, struck, reviled, and crucified out of love for us. You are indeed about to receive God Himself, in Whose hand is the destiny of the universe.

On the other hand, think of your own utter insignificance, and your vile sinfulness which has reduced you below the level of the brute, and made you worthy of being the sport and slave of devils. Consider your acknowledgment of the infinite favors you have received from your Saviour; you have insulted the Redeemer and trampled upon His precious blood, displaying a most arrant ingratitude.

But even human ingratitude cannot overcome divine charity; capricious fickleness is no match for unchanging love. Still the gracious Lord summons you to the divine banquet, and rather than rebuffing you for your obvious inadequacies, bids you come under pain of death. The arms of the merciful Father are always open to receive you, be you leprous, lame, blind, profligate, or possessed by devils. He demands of you these few requisites alone:

a. To be sincerely sorry for having so grievously offended Him.

b. To hate sin of all kind with an unquenchable vigor.

c. To consecrate yourself to cheerful acceptance of His divine will whatever it may be.

d. To have a firm confidence that He will forgive your sins, cleanse your soul of all taint, and defend you against all your enemies.

Encouraged by this ineffable love of the Lord for you and all penitent sinners, approach the holy table with a prudent fear, tempered by hope and love, saying:

"After so many grievous offenses, I am not worthy to receive Thee, not having fully satisfied Thy justice. No, my God, I am unworthy of Thee, sullied as I am by an inordinate attachment to creatures and a reluctance to serve Thee completely with my whole heart and my whole strength.

"O my omnipotent Lord, be mindful of Thy goodness and Thy promise; through the divine alchemy of love and faith, make my heart a worthy dwelling place for Thy divine Son."

After Communion strive to be deeply recollected, shutting out from your heart the multiple petty encroachments of worldly distractions. Entertain the divine guest with such sentiments as are expressed in the following prayer:

"O sovereign Lord of heaven, what has brought Thee from celestial heights to the depths of earthly hearts?" His answer will be simply, "Love."

And you must reply: "O eternal love, what is it you ask of me?" And He will answer again: "Nothing but love. I would have no other fire within thee but charity, the ardent flames of which will conquer the impure flames of passion, and make thee pleasing in My sight.

"Long have I wished that thou wert all Mine, and I all thine. And long have I desired that surrender of thy will ever solicitous for frivolous liberty and worldly vanities; for only when thy will is attuned to Mine can the first wish be realized.

"Know, then, that I would have thee die to self, that you might live to Me; I would have thee give Me thy heart that I might make it like unto Mine, which broke on Calvary out of love for mankind. Thou knowest who I am, and yet thou knowest that in some measure, I have made thee My equal in an excess of love. When I give Myself entirely to thee, I ask nothing but thyself in return. Be Mine and I shall be satisfied. Will nothing, think nothing, understand nothing, see nothing but Me and My will. Let thy nothingness be lost in the depths of My infinity, and find there thy happiness, as I find repose in thee."

Finally offer to the Eternal Father His only-begotten Son:

1. First in thanksgiving for the unspeakably

great favors He has rendered in bestowing them on you.

2. In petition for such things as are needed by you and those to whom you are obligated to pray; remember also in your petitions the souls in Purgatory.

Let this entire offering be made in commemoration of and in union with the offering made by Christ on Calvary's hill, when bleeding on the cross, He offered Himself to His Eternal Father.

Similarly, you may offer for the same intention, the sacrifice of the Mass, wherever it may be celebrated that day throughout the Christian world.

CHAPTER FIFTY-SIX

Concerning Spiritual Communion

ALTHOUGH ACTUAL RECEPTION of the sacrament of the Eucharist is limited to once a day, you are nevertheless at liberty to communicate in spirit every hour. And nothing except your own negligence can prevent you from receiving the inestimable benefits to be derived from such a union with Him. It is worth noting that spiritual communion is sometimes of greater benefit to the soul and more acceptable to God than many sacramental communions received with little preparation and less affection.

When, therefore, you are properly disposed to receive the Son of God spiritually, be assured that He is ready thus to come to you as food and nourishment.

By way of preparation, think of Jesus, and after contemplating the multitude of your offenses, declare to Him your sincere sorrow for them. Then, with profound respect and unshaking faith, beg Him to condescend graciously to enter your heart; entreat Him to replenish it with grace as a remedy against its inherent weaknesses, and as a shield against the violence of its enemies. Every time you succeed in mortifying your passions, or in performing an act of virtue, take that opportunity of preparing your heart for the Son of God, as He has commanded. Then, addressing yourself to Him, fervently beg the blessings of His presence, both as the physician of your soul and as its protector. Ask Him ever to dwell within your soul and so to take possession of it as to repel its would-be destroyers.

Recall too, your last sacramental communion, and inflamed with love for your Saviour, say to Him: "When, O God, shall I receive Thee again? When will that happy day return, when once again you will dwell within my heart?"

If, however, you desire to communicate spiritually with an increase of devotion, begin to prepare for it over night. Let every mortification and every act of virtue tend to make your soul a more fitting abode for His spiritual presence.

In the morning, as you awake, meditate upon the innumerable advantages to be derived from Holy Communion. Recall that the soul regains her lost virtues, recovers her pristine purity, and is rendered worthy to partake of the merits of the cross. The very reception of the sacrament is highly pleasing to the Eternal Father, Who desires everyone to enjoy this divine gift.

Later endeavor to excite within your soul an ardent desire of receiving Him in compliance with His holy will. Let your words match the sentiment as follows:

"O Lord, since I am not permitted the joy of Thy sacramental presence this day, let Thy goodness and omnipotence decree the cleansing of my soul from the stain of sin, that healed of my wounds, I may deserve to receive Thee in spirit. Every day and every hour, fortified anew by Thy grace, may I courageously resist my enemies, particularly that failing against which for the love of Thee, I wage unceasing war."

CHAPTER FIFTY-SEVEN

CONCERNING THANKSGIVING

SINCE ALL THE GOOD we have, or all the good we do, is of God and from God, we are bound in justice to render Him thanks for every good action done, or every victory won in the battle against self. And what is more, we are obliged to render thanks for all blessings, general or particular, which we have received from His bounteous hand.

To do this in a becoming manner, let us consider the end because of which He has heaped upon us the abundance of His blessings; for from such considerations we come to learn how God would be thanked. And as His principal design in all His beneficence is primarily His own honor and the dedication of souls to His divine service, let every one reflect within his hearts: "What power, wisdom and goodness has God displayed in bestowing this grace and blessing upon me!" Then considering the incapacity of finite man to merit unaided an infinite favor—or even man's utter ingratitude which makes him unworthy of such a blessing—we should say in deep humility:

"Is it possible, O Lord, that Thou shouldst love sinful man, the most abject of creatures? How boundless is a love which grants a multitude of blessings to him who deserves it so little! May Thy holy name be blessed now and forever!"

And finally, as such a multitude of blessings requires no more acknowledgment from man than that he love his gracious benefactor, let him thank and love God from the bottom of his heart, resolving to obey completely the dictates of God's holy will. The concluding step consists in the entire offering of self to God, as suggested in the following chapter.

CHAPTER FIFTY-EIGHT

THE OFFERING OF SELF TO GOD

THERE ARE TWO THINGS necessary to make our self-oblation completely acceptable to God. One is that it be made in union with the offering made by Christ to the Father; and the other is that it be totally free from all attachment to creatures.

1. As regards the first, we must remember that the Son of God, during His sojourn on earth, offered to His heavenly Father, not only Himself and His works, but also us and our works. Thus must our oblation be made in union with His, and dependent upon His, that both may be sanctified in the sight of the Almighty.

2. With regard to the second, we must remember that we can hardly offer ourselves to heaven, if we are bound to earth by worldly attachments. Therefore, if we perceive ourselves to be bound by the slightest earthly affection, let us have recourse to God, imploring Him to break asunder the bonds which chain us to earth that we may be His alone. This is of great importance. For if he who is a slave to creatures, pretends to give himself to God while bound to creatures, he gives what is not his, for he is the property of those creatures to whom he has given his will. To offer to God what has been given to creatures is to mock the Almighty. Thus it is that although we have offered ourselves as a holocaust to the Lord, yet

we have not only failed to advance in the way of virtue, but have even contracted fresh imperfections, and increased the number of our sins.

We may indeed offer ourselves to God while still attached to creatures, but it must be with the hope that His goodness will set us free, and that we may consecrate ourselves entirely to His service. Therefore let all our offerings be pure and untainted, destined to the honor of God alone. Let us be oblivious of the good things of both heaven and earth, having nothing in mind but the accomplishment of the will of God, and adoring His divine Providence. Let us sacrifice every affection of our souls to Him and, forgetting earthly things, let us say:

"Behold, O my God and Creator, the offering I make of my entire being—I submit my will entirely to thine; dispose of me as Thou wouldst in life and in death, in time or eternity."

If we make this prayer from the depths of our hearts, our sincerity will be tested in time of adversity, and we shall prove ourselves to be citizens of heaven, not of earth. We shall be children of God and He will be ours; for He dwells constantly with those who, renouncing themselves and all other creatures, offer themselves up as holocausts to His divine Majesty.

Here, then, you find a powerful means of vanquishing your enemies; for if, in uniting yourself to God, you become all His, and He all yours, what power or what enemy can ever harm you? And when you would offer fasting, prayers, acts

of patience, or good deeds, think first of the oblation of works, prayers, and fasts offered by Christ
to His Father, and place all confidence in their
infinite merit. But if we desire to offer to this
Father of Mercy the sufferings of His son in satisfaction for our sins, we may do so in the following manner:

1. First, we must call to mind, either in general
or particular, the chief disorders of our past lives;
and convinced of our inadequacy to appease the
divine wrath of our sovereign Judge, or satisfy
His offended justice, we must have recourse to the
life and passion of our Saviour. We must remember that when He prayed, fasted, labored, and
shed His precious blood, He offered all His acts
and sufferings to reconcile us with His Almighty
Father, saying, as it were: "Behold, O Eternal
Father, according to Thy will, how I comply with
Thy decrees in atoning for the sins of N. May it
please Thy divine Majesty to grant pardon to him
and graciously to receive him into the number of
Thy elect."

Everyone ought to join his prayers with those
of Jesus Christ, and implore the Eternal Father
to have mercy on him through the merits of the
passion and death of His Son. This may be done
every time we meditate on the life or passion of
Our Lord, not only in considering the individual
mysteries, but also the various circumstances of
each of the mysteries. The mode of oblation may
apply whether our prayers be offered up for self
or for others.

CHAPTER FIFTY-NINE

CONCERNING SENSIBLE DEVOTION AND DRYNESS

SENSIBLE DEVOTION is sometimes produced by dispositions of our nature, sometimes by artifices of the devil, and sometimes by an influx of grace. You may discern its origin in a particular case by studying the effects; for if no amendment follows, you may well suspect the devil or your own infirm nature to be at the bottom of such devotion, particularly if it be accompanied by much consolation, complacency, or by any measure of self-esteem.

When, therefore, your heart rejoices in exultation and spiritual delight, be not oversolicitous to trace their origins; but at the same time, attribute no particular significance to them, and beware of inflating your opinion of self. Rather, be ever mindful of your own nothingness, and breaking asunder the fetters of earthly attachments—and even spiritual attractions—attach yourself to God alone, seeking always to obey the least dictate of His divine will. This method of conduct will change the very nature of the consolation you experience, and although it should first arise from a defective source, it will later prove most beneficial.

Dryness, or spiritual aridity, proceeds from the following causes:

1. From the devil, who strives with satanic vigor to make us become negligent, to lead us from the path of perfection, and plunge us anew into the vanities of the world.

2. From ourselves, through our own faults, negligences and earthly attachments.

3. From the divine grace infused into our souls by the Holy Spirit, not only to wean us away from all that is not of God or tending to Him, but also that we may learn from experience that all things come from Him. Other reasons for such spiritual aridity are: to teach us to esteem His gifts more highly in the future, and show more humility and care in preserving them, and to unite us more closely to His divine Majesty by an entire renunciation of self, complete to the exclusion of spiritual comforts. For if our affections are centered on spiritual consolation, that heart which Our Lord would keep wholly for Himself is divided.

The last reason to be assigned for such dryness may be the joy God derives from seeing us fight with all our strength, utilizing all His grace to best effect.

When, therefore, you find yourself oppressed with dryness and distaste for spiritual things, ascertain whether or not it is to be attributed to any fault of your own, and if so, amend it instantly, not so much with a view to regaining that sensible enjoyment, but in order to banish everything that is the least displeasing to God. If, however, after careful scrutiny, you can discover no such fault, be not concerned about recovering your sensible fervor; rather exert yourself in the acquisition of that perfect devotion which consists in perfect conformity to the will of God. However barren and insipid your usual exercises may seem, be resolute and persevering in your execution of them, drinking cheerfully the bitter cup the heavenly Father has presented to you.

And if, besides this dryness which makes you almost insensible to heavenly things, you labor under an oppressive cloud of spiritual darkness which makes you fearful, and ignorant of which way to turn, be not discouraged. Let nothing separate you from the cross of Christ, and disdain all human consolation, vain and wretched as it is.

Be careful, moreover, not to divulge this affliction to anyone but your spiritual director, to whom it should be revealed not with a view to any alleviation, but in order to learn how to bear it in perfect resignation to the divine will. Offer not your Communions, prayers, or other devout exercises that you may be free of your cross, but that you may receive strength to exalt that cross forever to the honor and glory of Jesus crucified.

And if, from confusion of mind, you can neither pray nor meditate as usual, yet you must persist in those exercises with as little anxiety as possible, supplying for the defects of the mind the affection of the will. Employ vocal prayer, conversing both with yourself and your Saviour. Such a practice will have surprising effects, and it will afford you great consolation in your anxiety. On such occasions say to yourself: "Quare tristis es, anima mea, et quare conturbas me? Spera in Deo, quoniam adhuc confitebor illi, salutare vultus mei et Deus meus . . . Ut quid Domine, recessisti longe, despicis in opportunitate, in tribulatione? Non me derelinquas usquequaque."

Call to mind the pious sentiments with which God inspired Sara, the wife of Tobias, in her affliction, and say with her in spirit and in word:

> "My God, all who serve Thee know that if they are visited with trials of affliction in this life, they will be rewarded; if oppressed with affliction they shall be delivered: if punished by Thy justice, they hope in mercy. For Thou delightest not in seeing us perish; Thou sendest a calm after storms, and joy after mourning. O God of Israel, be Thy name forever blessed." (Tob. III)

Remember also thy Christ in the garden and on the cross abandoned by Him whose only beloved Son He was; carry your cross with Him and say from the bottom of your heart: "Not my will but thine be done."

Thus by uniting patience with prayer in the voluntary immolation of self to God, you will become truly devout. For, as I have said, true devotion consists in an eager and unswerving will to follow Christ, and to bear the cross at whatever time, in whatever way He shall decide; and it consists too in loving God because He is worthy of our love, and even in forfeiting the sweetness of God for the sake of God.

If the multitudes of those who profess piety would measure advancement in the spiritual life by this true standard, rather than by the saccharine effervescences of a purely sensible devotion, they would be deceived neither by the devil nor by themselves; nor would they be so abominably ungrateful as to murmur against their Lord, and unjustly complain of the gift He bestows upon them. For such situations in which the virtue of patience may be developed and strengthened are truly gifts. On the contrary, these multitudes would exert themselves in serving Him with greater fidelity than ever, being convinced that He permits everything for the greater advancement of His glory and our salvation.

There is another dangerous illusion to which women especially are frequently subject, detesting vice as they do and being sedulously watchful in avoiding occasions of sin. At times, as they are molested by impure and frightful thoughts and even loathsome visions, they become despondent, thinking that God has forsaken them. They cannot conceive of the Holy Spirit dwelling in a soul filled with impure thoughts, and imagine themselves inevitably banished from the divine presence.

Being thus disheartened, they are ready to despair, and half-conquered by the temptation, they think of forsaking their exercises of devotion entirely and returning to Egypt. Blind as they are, they do not see God's goodness in permitting them to be tempted as a preventive measure against human negligence, and also a coercive measure designed to bring prodigal man to closer union with his loving Father. Actually, therefore, it is most thoughtless for them to complain of that which should occasion their unceasing gratitude.

On such occasions, we should consider well the perverse propensities of our wounded nature. For God, Who knows best what is to our ultimate advantage, would make us aware that of ourselves we tend to nothing but sin, and when unaided by Him, fall into innumerable miseries.

After this, we must cultivate within ourselves a loving confidence in His divine mercy, realizing that since He has been pleased to open our eyes to our danger, He also wishes to free us from it and join us to Him in prayer and confidence; for this we owe Him our most humble thanks.

To advert again to those vile thoughts which are involuntary; it is certain that they are put to flight much sooner by a patient resignation to the anxiety they occasion, and a speedy application of the mind to something else, than by a tumultuous and overanxious resistance.

CHAPTER SIXTY

CONCERNING THE EXAMINATION OF CONSCIENCE

IN THE EXAMINATION of conscience, consider three things:

1. The faults committed on the particular day.

2. The occasions of these faults.

3. Your need of alacrity in amending those faults and acquiring the contrary virtues.

With regard to the faults committed each day, recall the recommendations of Chapter Twenty-Six, which treats of the mode of behavior to be adopted by one who has fallen into sin. It goes without saying that you must strive with the greatest caution and circumspection to avoid the occasions of these faults. And as to the amendment of these faults and the acquisition of the requisite virtues, you must fortify your will by a firm confidence in God, Who will aid you in remedying the evil habits.

If, however, you find that you have triumphed in the struggle over self or excelled in the performance of a good work, beware of vainglory. Even the memory of such victories should not be too much in your thoughts, lest presumption and vanity steal quietly and insidiously into your heart. Leave, therefore, your good works, whatever they may be, to the mercy of God and, forgetting the triumphs of the past, fortify yourself for the struggles of the future.

As to your thanksgiving for the gifts and favors which the Lord has bestowed upon you in the course of the day, humbly acknowledge Him to be the author of all good, and your protector against myriad unseen foes. Thank Him for having inspired you with good thoughts and for having given you the opportunities of practicing virtue. And finally, thank Him for all His unknown gifts of which you will never know.

CHAPTER SIXTY-ONE

Concerning the Manner in Which We Are to Persevere in the Spiritual Combat Until Death

ONE OF THE REQUISITES in the spiritual combat is perseverance in the continual mortification of our unruly passions; for never in this life are they utterly subdued, but take root in the human heart like weeds in fertile soil. This is a battle from which we cannot escape; ours is a foe we cannot evade. The fight against passion will last a lifetime, and he who lays down his arms will be slain.

Moreover, we must combat enemies who hate us with unquenchable fury, and are consecrated to our destruction. The more we would make friends of them, the more they would make derelicts of us.

But be not daunted by their strength or number, for in this war, he alone is conquered who voluntarily surrenders, and the entire power of our enemies is in the hands of that captain under whose banner we fight. And not only will He preserve us from treachery, but He will be our champion. He who is infinitely superior to all the foe will crown you with conquest provided that you, as a warrior, rely not on your own finite powers, but on His almighty power and infinite goodness.

If, however, He seems slow in coming to your aid and apparently leaves you in the withering fire of the enemy, be not discouraged; rather fight resolutely in the firm belief that He will convert all things which befall you to your eventual benefit, and even the unexpected crown of victory will be yours.

For your part, never desert your commanding officer, who, for your sake, did not shrink from death itself, and in dying on Calvary's hill, conquered the entire world. Fight courageously under His colors, and lay not down your arms while there is one foe left. For if a single vice is neglected it will be a beam in your eye, and a thorn in your side, constantly hindering you from triumph in your glorious and victorious cause.

CHAPTER SIXTY-TWO

CONCERNING OUR PREPARATION AGAINST THE ENEMIES WHO ASSAIL US AT THE HOUR OF DEATH

ALTHOUGH OUR ENTIRE LIFE on earth is a continual warfare, it is certain that the last day of battle will be the most dangerous; for he who falls on this day, falls never to rise again.

In order, therefore, to be prepared, we must prepare ourselves now; for he who fights well through life will with greater facility emerge victorious in the final assault. Meditate too on death, considering its significance, for such consideration will remove the terror that strikes when death is nigh, and give your mind greater freedom for the combat.

Worldly men cannot stand the thought of death; they refuse to think of it lest they be distracted from the earthly pleasures in which they have placed their affection. The thought of losing transient things is naturally repugnant and painful to one who is oblivious to eternal things. Thus the affections of worldlings are more firmly riveted to this world day by day. And day by day the contemplation of the loss of worldly things strikes increased terror most frequently into the hearts of those who have enjoyed worldliness the longest.

In order to be prepared for the awesome step

from time into eternity, imagine yourself sometime all alone in the face of the agonies of death, and consider the things that would most likely trouble you at that hour. Then imprint deeply in your heart the remedies I shall propose to be employed when the situation is at hand. For the blow that can be struck but once should be well-rehearsed, as a final error means an eternity of regret and misery.

CHAPTER SIXTY-THREE

CONCERNING THE FOUR ASSAULTS OF THE
ENEMY AT THE HOUR OF DEATH. THE FIRST
ASSAULT AGAINST FAITH AND THE MANNER
OF RESISTING IT

THERE ARE FOUR principal assaults to which the enemy is likely to resort when we are at the threshold of death. They are temptations against faith and to despair, thoughts of vainglory, and finally, various illusions employed by the children of darkness, who are disguised as angels of light.

As to the first assault, depend rather on the will than on the understanding, saying: "Get thee behind me, Satan, father of lies, for I will not even hear thee; it is enough for me to believe as the Holy Catholic Church believes."

Similarly, be sedulously watchful against any thoughts which may appear to be conducive to the strengthening of your faith; reject them instantly as suggestions of the devil, who seeks desperately to lure you into dispute. If, however, you find it impossible to turn your thoughts resolutely from such matters, at least be adamant in your refusal to listen to Scriptural quotations the adversary may glibly present; for although they are apparently clear and precise, they will be invariably garbled, misinterpreted, or incorrectly applied.

If, at this time, the evil one asks what the Church believes, ignore him; but seeing his aim is to surprise or entrap you in words, be content with making a general act of faith. If you wish to mortify him further, answer that the Church believes the truth; and if he wishes to know what truth is, tell him it is what the Church believes and teaches.

Above all, keep your heart intently fixed on Jesus crucified, saying: "My God, My Creator and Redeemer, hurry to my assistance, and stay with me lest I wander from the truth which Thou hast taught me. Grant that as I was born in the faith, so may I die in the faith to Thy glory and my salvation!"

CHAPTER SIXTY-FOUR

CONCERNING THE ASSAULT OF DESPAIR AND ITS REMEDY

THE SECOND ASSAULT by which the perverse one attempts our destruction is the terror which he would infuse into our minds at the recollection of our past sins, hoping thereby to drive us to despair.

In this peril, hold fast to the infallible rule that the remembrance of your sins is the effect of grace, and is most salutary if it inspires within your heart sentiments of humility, compunction, and confidence in God's mercy. But if such recollection creates vexation and despondency, leaving you spiritless from the apparent cogency of the reasons adduced to convince you that you are irrevocably lost, be assured that it has been suggested by the devil. In such circumstances, humble yourself the more, and have greater confidence in God; thus shall you destroy the strategem of the devil, turn his own weapons against him, and give greater glory to God.

It is true that you should be truly contrite for having offended such sovereign goodness, as often as you call to mind your past offenses; but as often as you ask pardon you should have a firm confidence in the infinite mercy of Jesus Christ.

I will go further and say that even though God

Himself should seem to say within your heart that you are not one of His flock, still place your confidence in Him; rather say to Him in all humility: "Thou hast good reason indeed, O Lord, to condemn me for my sins, but I have greater reason in Thy mercy to hope for pardon. Have pity then, O Lord, on a humble sinner condemned by his own sinfulness, but redeemed by your blood. I commit myself entirely to Thy hands, O my Redeemer; all my hopes are in Thee, trusting that in Thy infinite compassion, Thou will save me to the glory of Thy name. Do with me as Thou wilt, for Thou alone art my Lord. Even though, My Lord, Thou shouldst destroy me, ever will I hope in Thee."

CHAPTER SIXTY-FIVE

CONCERNING TEMPTATION TO VAINGLORY

THE THIRD ASSAULT is that of vainglory and presumption. Dread nothing so much as yielding in the least way to an exalted opinion of your person or your good works. Take no glory but in the Lord, and acknowledge that all that you are or ever hope to be is to be attributed to the merits of the life and death of Jesus Christ. Until the very evensong of life, hear nothing within your heart but the refrain of your own nothingness. Let your humility deepen as self-love fades, and unceasingly thank God, the Author of all your greatness. Stand ever in a holy and prudent fear, and acknowledge simply that all your endeavors are vain, unless God, in Whom is all your hope, crowns them with success.

If you will follow this advice, never shall your enemy prevail against you; your road will be open before you, and you may pass on joyfully to the heavenly Jerusalem.

CHAPTER SIXTY-SIX

Concerning the Various Illusions Employed by the Devil at the Hour of our Death

IF OUR PERSISTENT FOE, who never ceases to persecute us, should assail us disguised as an angel of light, stand firm and steadfast even though cognizant of your own nothingness, and say to him boldly: "Return, miserable one into your realms of darkness; for I am unworthy of visions, nor do I need anything but the mercy of my Saviour, and the prayers of Mary, Joseph and all the saints."

And though these visions seem to bear many evidences of having been born in heaven, still reject them as far as it is within your power to do so. And have no fear that this resistance, founded as it is on your own worthiness, will be displeasing to God. For if the vision be from Him, He has the power to make the same known to you, and you will suffer no detriment; for He who give grace to the humble does not withdraw it because of acts which spring from humility.

These, then, are the weapons which the enemy most commonly employs against us at the hour of our death. Each individual is tempted according to the particular inclination to which he is most subject. Therefore, before the zero hour of the great conflict, we should arm ourselves securely, and struggle manfully against our most violent passions, that the victory may be easier in that hour which leaves no future time for preparation or resistance.

"THOU SHALT FIGHT AGAINST THEM UNTIL THEY BE UTTERLY DESTROYED."—*I Kings 15:18.*

TREATISE ON PEACE OF SOUL AND INNER HAPPINESS

Of the soul which dies to self in order to live to God

CHAPTER ONE

The Nature of the Human Heart and the Way in Which It Should Be Governed

God created the heart of man for no other end than to love Him, and to be loved by Him; and the sublimity of this divine design should convince us that it is the noblest of the works of His almighty hand. Our first obligation, then, is to direct that heart to place its affection in proper things, that exterior acts might flow from interior dispositions of the heart. For although corporal penances and various chastisements of the flesh are praiseworthy when practiced in prudent moderation, yet by this means alone rather than acquiring a single virtue, you will probably acquire conceit and vanity. All externals will prove ineffectual unless they be invigorated by and permeated with worthy internal dispositions.

The life of man is nothing but a continual warfare and temptation; and because it is a warfare, you must watch over your heart with sedulous care that it may be ever at peace. If any movements signal sensual disturbances, take heed to calm the storms within your heart instantly, never permitting the pursuit of vain and illusory pleasures. Exercise this caution not only in time of prayer, but anytime disquieting thoughts assail you, for prayers will be indifferently said until the soul knows peace.

Observe, however, that all this must be done with a certain mildness and effortless ease, as the principal effort of our lives should be the quieting of our hearts, and the prudent guidance of those hearts lest they go astray.

CHAPTER TWO

THE CARE TO BE EXERCISED BY THE SOUL IN THE ACQUISITION OF PERFECT TRANQUILLITY

THE MILD, peaceful, constant attention to the feelings of the heart will produce wonderful results; for we shall not only pray and act with great facility and peace, but shall even suffer without lamenting the disturbing elements of contempt and the injuries themselves.

It is necessary, however, to undergo much toil before we acquire this serenity, for our inexperience inevitably exposes us to the assaults of powerful enemies. But once acquired, this peace will bring untold consolation to our souls in their fight against the disquieting elements of the world, and daily we shall perfect the art of quieting the turmoil of the spirit.

If at times you are in such confusion of mind that you seem totally incapable of calming yourself, have immediate recourse to prayer. And persevere in it in imitation of Christ, Our Lord, Who prayed three times in the garden to show mankind that only in conversation with God can afflicted souls find haven and refuge.

Let us pray without ceasing that repose may replace the chaos in our hearts, and that a humble submissiveness to God's will may bring our soul to its former tranquillity.

Let us not be disturbed by the endless and pointless hurry of the business world; when we are at work, let us attend to business affairs with composure and ease, refraining from rigid conformity to a harsh, exacting schedule, and too great an eagerness to see our work done.

Our principal intention, a continual awareness of God's holy presence, and an unchanging desire to please Him, should preside over all our actions. And if we permit any other consideration to interfere, our souls will soon abound with fear and anxiety; we shall often fall, and the difficulty of recovering will convince us that our evils proceed invariably from acting in compliance with our own will and inclination. If on such occasions we are successful, then we are puffed up with vain satisfaction; and if we are disappointed, we are overwhelmed by uneasiness and vexation.

CHAPTER THREE

The Necessity of Building This Peaceful Habitation by Degrees

BANISH FROM YOUR MIND whatever tends to depress and disconcert you, striving always with great mildness to acquire or preserve serenity of soul. For Christ Himself has said: "Blessed are the peacemakers . . . Learn of me for I am meek and humble of heart." Never doubt that God will crown your labor and make your soul a dwelling of delight; all He asks of you is a sincere attempt to disperse the clouds and storms whenever you are molested by disturbances of the senses and passions, that the sun of peace may shine on all your actions.

As a house cannot be built in a day, neither can the mansion of inner peace be built within our souls in a fleeting instant. Rather, our success is a gradual attainment; it is the culmination of the primary work of the divine architect in predisposing our souls for the edifice to be built therein, and the firm establishment of humility which must be the foundation of that edifice.

CHAPTER FOUR

THE NECESSITY OF RELINQUISHING HUMAN CONSOLATIONS IN THE ACQUISITION OF INNER PEACE

THE PATH WHICH LEADS to this heavenly peace is almost unknown to the world. For along that path tribulations and trials are sought with the same avidity that the worldling displays in the pursuit of pleasure. There contempt and derision are pursued as are honors and glory by the ambitious; there as great pains are taken to neglect and be neglected, to forsake and be forsaken, as the children of this world take to be sought for, caressed, and admired by the mighty and the rich. And there holy ambition is known, comforted, and favored by God alone.

The Christian soul, as it travels this path, learns to converse with God alone and to be so strongly fortified by His presence, that it is willing to suffer anything for Him and the promotion of His glory.

There one learns that suffering blots out the sun, and that affliction endured in the proper manner is a treasure laid up for eternity; and there one learns too that to suffer with Jesus Christ is the only ambition of the soul which seeks the glory of resembling Him.

There one is taught that to love ourselves, to follow our own wills, to obey our sensual appetites, and to destroy ourselves are one and the same thing. There one is taught too that our own will is not even to be gratified in what is commendable, until we have submitted it in all simplicity and humility of heart to the will of God; that what He ordains and not what we wish should be the rule of our actions.

Frequently we perform good works from wrong motives, or through indiscreet zeal, which, like the false prophet, appears to be an innocent lamb, when in reality it is a ravenous wolf. The devout soul, however, will discover the illusion from the effects produced. When it finds itself in trouble and anxiety, humility diminished and composure disturbed; when it no longer enjoys peace and tranquillity, and perceives all that has been attained with much time and labor to be lost—then the fact is really fantasy.

We may sometimes fall on the path to inner peace; but this only serves to increase humility which assists us to recover and to watch more strictly over ourselves in the future. Perhaps God permits us to fall in order to root out some secret fault, artfully concealed by our deceitful self-love.

Sometimes, too, the soul may be molested with temptations to sin, but it must not be unduly disturbed on this account; rather must the soul quietly withdraw from such temptations, reinstating itself in its former tranquillity without indulging in an excess of either joy or sorrow.

In a word, all we must do is to keep our souls in purity and peace in the sight of God, knowing by experience that He ordains everything for our ultimate welfare.

CHAPTER FIVE

The Necessity of Keeping the Soul Disengaged and in Solitude That God's Holy Will May Operate in It

IF WE ARE TRULY cognizant of the priceless worth of the immortal soul, that sublime temple of God Himself, let us take care that nothing of the world intrude therein. Placing our hope in the Lord, we should wait with a firm confidence for His coming, and realize that He will certainly enter the soul unattached to worldly things and ready to receive Him alone. Alone, having no desire but the presence of God; alone, loving only Him; alone, void of all will but the will of heaven.

Let us learn to do nothing to please ourselves, that we may merit in the soul of the human the presence of the divine, the comprehension of Whom is far beyond the horizons of created intellects.

Let us follow exactly the prescriptions of our spiritual father and of those who govern us in the place of God, that every suffering and good work offered to God may be prudent and salutary.

It is sufficient that we keep ourselves ever ready and willing to suffer for love of Him all that He wills and the manner in which He wills it. Whoever acts solely in conjunction with the dictates of his own will would do much better were he to remain in peace, attentive to what God wills to perform in him. Therefore, we must always avoid attachments of the will which should ever be free and in perfect harmony with the divine.

And since we ought not to act according to our desires, let us not consciously attach our wills to any one thing; but if we should desire something, let it be in such a way as to leave us as unperturbed as if we had desired nothing, should our desire fail to materialize.

For our desires are our chains, and to be entangled in them is to be a slave. To free ourselves from desires, therefore, is to free ourselves from tyranny.

God demands that our souls be alone and unattached that He may manifest His manifold wonders in them, glorifying them even in this life by His divine power.

O Holy Solitude! O desert of happiness! O glorious hermitage, where a soul may find its God! Let us not only run to such an exalted place, but beg the wings of a dove that we may fly to it and find there a holy repose. Let us not stop by the wayside; let us not tarry on the way for frivolous conversation; let us leave the dead to bury their dead, forsaking the land of the lifeless for the land of the living.

CHAPTER SIX

The Necessity of Our Love of Neighbor Being Guided by Prudence That Serenity of Soul Be Not Disturbed

GOD DOES NOT DWELL in a soul which He does not first inflame with a love of Him and charity for others; for Christ Himself said He came to set the world on fire.

Although our love of God must have no bounds, our charity for our neighbor must have its limits. We cannot love our God too much, but if our love for others is not guided by prudent moderation, we may destroy ourselves in seeking to save others.

Let us, therefore, love our neighbor in a manner which will not be deleterious to our own souls; this is best accomplished by doing nothing with the sole aim of setting them a good example, lest in saving them we lose ourselves. Rather our actions should be performed with great simplicity and sanctity, with the sole aim of pleasing God in humble acknowledgment of the limited value of our good works to ourselves and others. We are not expected to be so zealous for the salvation of others, as to destroy the peace of our own souls.

We may ardently desire their illumination when God is pleased that we do so; but we must not wait for a divine communication nor vainly imagine that it is to be acquired by our exaggerated solicitude and imprudent zeal.

Let us seek the peace and repose of a holy solitude, for such is the will of God as it binds us closer to Him; and let us remain recollected and undisturbed until the lord of the vineyard requires our services. God will clothe us with Himself when He finds us divested of all earthly care and solicitude.

When we have forgotten ourselves, God will not forget us; peace will reign in our hearts, and divine love will grant us an undisturbed facility of action, as well as moderation and temperance in all that we do. Thus every action of our lives shall be performed in the repose of a heaven-sent peace in which even silence is eloquent; and to be free of earthly care in order to offer ourselves to the service of the Master is to act in accordance with the will of Christ. For it is His divine goodness that must work in us and with us, requiring no more of us than sufficient humility to present to Him a soul that has but one desire, and this desire is that God's will be accomplished in us in the most perfect possible manner.

CHAPTER SEVEN

The Necessity of Divesting Our Souls Entirely of Their Own Will, That They May Be Presented to God

"Come to me all ye that labor and are burdened, and I will refresh you . . . all you that thirst, come to the fountain." Such are the words of Christ in the Scriptures; let us follow this divine summons, without impulsiveness or clamor, in peace and mildness, referring ourselves respectfully and confidently to our loving and omnipotent God.

Let us wait calmly for the coming of that spirit which brings peace; let us, entirely resigned and obedient to the decrees of His holy will, think of nothing but the means by which He may be desired, loved and glorified.

Let these acts be performed without using force or violence on our hearts, lest by an unwise use of these instruments, our souls be rendered incapable of that sweet repose, which on this earth is their glory.

Rather let us gradually accustom our souls to contemplate nothing but the love and goodness of God; let them be ever mindful of the heavenly manna with which they shall be nourished in ineffable sweetness, once they accustom themselves to frequent meditation on these sublime truths.

Avoid shedding useless tears or striving to excite within yourself an emotional display of devotion; but abide quietly in interior solitude until the will of God is accomplished in you. And when He gives you tears, they shall be sweet and effortless; accept them with gentleness and serenity, and above all with humility. By these indications shall you ascertain the source from which they spring, receiving them as dew from heaven itself.

Let us not presume to know, have, or desire particular things, for the very cornerstone of the spiritual edifice is not dependent on our knowledge, possessions, or desires in the slightest degree. Rather should we remain in a state of perfect self-denial like Mary at the feet of Jesus, instead of busying ourselves with many things like Martha.

When you seek God by the light of your human understanding, you must avoid purely human concepts, or comparisons which limit, or inadvertently circumscribe His unbounded greatness. For He is beyond all comparison; He is beyond all division, He is omnipresent, containing all things in Himself.

Try to visualize a limitless immensity, a unity which really defies human comprehension, and a power which has created and sustains all things in the entire universe in a feat of inimitable grandeur. Then say humbly within your soul: "Behold thy God."

Contemplate and admire Him unceasingly in all times and in all places, for as He is everywhere, He is in your soul, and in it He rejoices as He has said. And although the Almighty stands in not the slightest need of your soul, He is pleased to make it a worthy habitation of Himself.

In your intellectual pursuit of these sublime truths, be sure to retain a calm and peaceful will. Strive not to limit yourself to so many prayers, meditations, or readings, neither neglect nor limit your customary devotions. Rather let your heart be at liberty to stop where it finds its God, having no misgivings about unfinished exercises if He is pleased to communicate Himself to you in the midst of them. Have no scruples in this regard, for the end of your devotion is to enjoy God, and as the end is accomplished, the means have no significance for the present.

God leads us by the path that He has chosen, and if we oblige ourselves to precise execution of exercises which we fancy, we are imposing imaginary obligations on ourselves; and far from finding God, we are actually running away from Him, pretending to please Him, yet not conforming to His holy will.

If you really desire to advance successfully on this path, and attain the end to which it leads, seek and desire God alone; and whenever and wherever you find Him, there stop, go no farther. While God dwells with you enjoy His company with the celestial peace of saints; and when His divine majesty pleases to retire, then turn again to the quest of your God in your devout exercises.

This advice is of the greatest importance and well merits our attention. For frequently we see many clerics who exhaust themselves in the fatiguing execution of their duties without deriving any advantages for themselves, or finding peace. For they imagine they have done nothing if they leave their task unfinished, believing perfection to consist in constant adherence to the minutest prescriptions of their own wills. Thus their lives are spent in weariness and toil as one who labors fruitlessly through the years; never do they obtain that true repose and interior peace in which the Lord truly dwells, for it is the peaceful soul that is a sanctuary of Jesus Christ.

CHAPTER EIGHT

Concerning Our Faith in the Blessed Sacrament, and the Method by Which We are to Offer Ourselves to God

Our faith and love in the Holy Eucharist must so increase and strengthen as to become almost part of the very fibre of our being. Such faith and love cannot be successfully cultivated without a disciplined will, prepared to undergo all afflictions, tribulations, infirmities, and spiritual dryness for the sake of Jesus Christ. It is not for us to ask Him to change Himself into us, rather should we humbly petition to be changed into Him.

Entertain Him not with pompous speeches or empty words. Admiration and exultation should so engulf our souls as to submerge these functions, as it were, when He is present. Our understanding should be completely absorbed in joyous contemplation of this incomprehensible mystery, and our heart suffused with joy at the sight of such immense majesty under such simple appearances. And let us desire no further manifestation of His divinity, remembering His deathless words: "Blessed are they who have not seen, and have believed."

Above all let us be constant and punctual in our devotions, and practice unceasingly those means most conducive to purifying and adorning our souls with a peaceful and mild simplicity. And while these methods are followed, the grace of perseverance will never be wanting to us.

A soul which has once known the ineffable delight of spiritual peace can never return to the hurry and confusion of a worldly life; for it is impossible for her to endure it in such circumstances.

CHAPTER NINE

TRUE HAPPINESS IS NOT TO BE FOUND IN PLEASURE OR COMFORT, BUT IN GOD ALONE

A SOUL WHICH IS deliberately oblivious of the goods of this world, but relishes its mortifications and persecutions, which neither loves all it can bestow nor dreads all it can inflict, which avoids honors as it would a contagion, and cherishes humiliation as a beloved thing—such a soul may expect all consolation from God, provided it relies on the strength of God rather than on the weakness of self.

The courage of St. Peter was very great when he declared his resolution of dying with Christ, and his will apparently strong enough to merit commendation, but in reality Peter's reliance was a reliance on his own will, and this was the occasion of his shameful fall. How true it is that we can neither propose nor execute good, unless supported by the almighty power of God.

Let us purge our soul of all desires that nothing may impede its operations in the particular situation. This is not to say that one must ignore temporal affairs entirely, for they are to be managed with a prudent and commendable solicitude in accordance with the circumstances of the individual. Such management of temporal affairs is completely in harmony with the divine will, and is in no way at variance with our inner peace of soul and spiritual advancement.

We can do nothing better towards profitable employment of the particular time than to offer the soul, entirely divested of all desires, to almighty God, standing humbly before Him as a miserable culprit, incapable of doing anything for himself.

In this freedom of mind and disengagement of self in which there is utter dependence on God alone, we find the essence of perfection. And it is impossible to conceive how God loves and blesses those who have unselfishly consecrated themselves to Him completely. He is pleased to receive confidence without reserve, and he delights in enlightening them, in resolving their difficulties, in forgiving the offenses of the truly penitent, and in raising them when fallen.

For God is still the priest forever, and though He has given to St. Peter and his successors the power of loosing and binding, He has not divested Himself of those powers. So if the penitent cannot have recourse to their confessors as often as they wish, the divine majesty receives them in His infinite mercy, pardoning their sins whenever they approach Him with true confidence, perfect sorrow, and entire love. Such are the fruits of this detachment from self.

CHAPTER TEN

THE NECESSITY OF NOT BEING DEJECTED AT THE OBSTACLES AND REPUGNANCE WE FIND IN THE ACQUISITION OF THIS INTERIOR PEACE

GOD IS OFTEN PLEASED to permit our inner serenity, this solitude and holy peace of soul, to be disturbed and overcast with the clouds and emotions arising from our self-love and natural inclinations.

But as His goodness permits these trials for our greater good, He will not fail to bestow the refreshing showers of His divine consolation on this dryness of spirit, enriching the soul with the fruits and flowers of His undying love.

These interruptions of our tranquillity occasioned by the emotions of the sensitive appetites are the very combats in which the saints gained victories which merited them immortal crowns.

Whenever you fall into such weakness, disgust and desolation of spirit, say to God with an humble and affectionate heart: "Lord, I am the work of Thy hands and the slave redeemed by Thy precious blood; dispose of me as entirely Thine, made for Thee alone, and grant that my only hope may be in Thee." Thrice happy is the soul which thus offers itself to God in time of affliction!

Perhaps under particular circumstances you find yourself unable to bend your will immediately to an entire submission to God; if such is the case, you should not be dejected, for it is the cross the Master has commanded you to bear as you follow Him. Did He not first bear the cross of Golgotha to show you how to bear your little cross of earthly affliction? Contemplate His combat in the garden when He struggled with His human nature, the weakness of which made Him cry out: "Father, if it is possible, let this cup pass away from Me." And remember the soul that rose above the weakness of the body, to cry out in profound humility: "Not My will but Thine be done."

Perhaps the weakness of human nature may make you try to avoid all trouble or affliction, and at such times you may show your dislike which prompts you to keep suffering at a distance.

Nevertheless, be sure you persevere in prayer and acts of humility until you find no other desire or inclination than the accomplishment of God's holy will in your soul.

Try to keep your heart reserved for God alone, that there may be no room for bitterness, gall, or voluntary repugnance to what God shall appoint. Never be absorbed in the failings of others, but pursue your own path, regarding nothing but that which may wound your conscience. The great secret of belonging to God is to neglect and pass by everything else.

CHAPTER ELEVEN

CONCERNING THE ARTIFICES OF THE DEVIL TO DESTROY OUR PEACE OF SOUL, AND THE METHOD OF COMBATING THEM

THE ENEMY OF MANKIND endeavours chiefly to withdraw us from a state of humility and Christian simplicity by suggesting to us our superiority over others; this is soon followed by our manifestation of a critical attitude, and a contemptuous regard of the failings of others. The greatest means utilized by the evil one in stealing into our souls, however, is our own vanity and self-love; and the art of defeating him is to keep deeply entrenched in holy humility without ever forsaking it. If we do not attempt to so discipline self, we abandon ourselves to the proud spirit for whom we are no match. And once he gets possession of our wills, he plays the tyrant to perfection, introducing every vice into our souls.

It is not sufficient that we watch; we must also pray. For it has been said that we must watch and pray, and peace of mind is a treasure which cannot be secured unless it is thus guarded.

Let us not suffer our minds to be afflicted or disturbed on any account whatever. The humble and peaceful soul does everything with a facility that vaults over obstacles with grace and ease; its conduct is holy and the soul perseveres in it. But the soul which permits itself to be perturbed performs few good actions of any significance, and suffers continually but to no advantage.

You will discern whether thoughts are to be encouraged or banished by the confidence or diffidence they inspire in the divine mercy. If they suggest the continual increase of affectionate confidence, you are to look upon them as messengers from heaven, entertaining them and delighting in them. But you are to banish as the suggestion of hell itself all thoughts that make you the least diffident of His infinite goodness.

The tempter of pious souls often magnifies their imperfections, persuading the faithful that they are unfaithful to their duties, imperfect in confessions, tepid at communion, and deficient in prayer. Thus with various scruples he keeps them in constant alarm, seeking to distract them from their exercises, as if God had forgotten or forsaken them. Nothing can be more false than to believe this, for the advantages arising from distractions, spiritual dryness, and the like, are innumerable, provided the soul comprehends and complies with what God expects of her in those circumstances. And God only expects patience and perseverance. For the prayers and exercises of a soul, deprived of all satisfaction in what she does, is the delight of the Almighty, according to St. Gregory.

Particularly is such a soul pleasing to God if, notwithstanding its insensibility and apathy, it persists with courage. For the patience of such a soul is a prayer in itself, prevailing more with God than any prayers said with great emotional fervor. St. Gregory adds that the interior darkness with which her devotion is surrounded shines brightly in the presence of God, and that nothing we do can sooner draw us to Him or evoke from Him fresh gifts of grace.

Never forsake, therefore, any work of piety, however disinclined religiously you may be, unless you would comply with the wishes of Satan. Learn from the following chapter, the innumerable advantages to be reaped through a humble perseverance in works of piety, when attended with the most irksome spiritual barrenness.

CHAPTER TWELVE

The Necessity of Preserving Equanimity of Soul in the Midst of Internal Temptations

SPIRITUAL BARRENNESS and aridity bestow innumerable benefits upon the soul if accepted in the proper spirit of humility and patience. The thorough mastery of this secret would indeed prevent many uneasy days and unhappy hours of perturbation of spirit.

How utterly mistaken we are in thinking ourselves forsaken and abhorred by God Almighty, and deprived of the treasured tokens of His divine love; how erroneous to fancy ourselves punished by His anger, when actually we are favored by His goodness. Can we not see that the uneasiness which arises from such interior aridity can only spring from a desire of being altogether acceptable to God and zealous and fervent in His service? Such uneasiness rarely happens at the beginning of one's conversion to the service of God; rather it is found in those who have already consecrated themselves for some time to the Master, and are resolved to travel the paths of perfection.

On the contrary, we seldom hear the inveterate sinner or the worldling complain of such temptations. Thus we may well believe that these trials constitute a precious food by which God nourishes those whom He loves. Even though the temptation is so violent as to strike terror into our hearts, we shall derive innumerable blessings from it; for the blessing derived will be in proportion to the severity of our trial.

Such a situation the soul does not always understand, and shrinks from the path of crosses and afflictions. This is simply to say that the soul is unwilling to be deprived of delight and consolation, and whatever devotion is not accompanied by an emotional glow, so to speak, is erroneously esteemed to be no better than lost labor.

CHAPTER THIRTEEN

GOD PERMITS TEMPTATIONS FOR OUR ULTIMATE WELFARE

WE ARE by nature proud, ambitious, and ever mindful to the whims of our sense appetites. Hence it is that we are apt to flatter ourselves continually, and esteem ourselves out of all proportion to our merit.

Such presumption is so great an obstacle to our spiritual progress, that the slightest taint of it impedes us in the attainment of true perfection. It is an evil which we do not always discern, but God, Who loves us and knows the true viciousness of presumption, is watchful in rescuing us from this deceit, waking us from the lethargy of self-love and bringing us to true self-knowledge.

Did He not once rescue the erring Peter when He permitted that apostle to deny Him, and forswear any knowledge of his Lord? Did He not grant to Peter self-knowledge and strength to cast aside his dangerous presumption? Did He not similarly deal with St. Paul when, in order to preserve him from this insidious vice and prevent him from making an improper use of the sublime revelations intrusted to him, He permitted a troublesome temptation to constantly remind the Apostle of his weakness?

Let us admire, then, the beneficence and wisdom of God, Who so treats us for our own good, favoring us imperceptibly, even when we imagine He is afflicting us.

We are perhaps prone to attribute our tepidity to our imperfections, and our emotional apathy toward the things of God; and we are easily persuaded that no one is so distracted or forsaken as ourselves, that God has no servants as wretched as we are, and that none but miscreants have their minds filled with thoughts like ours.

Thus by the effects of this heavenly medicine is the patient, once swollen with presumption, reduced in his own opinion to the status of an unworthy Christian.

Would such a transformation ever happen were man left to his own devices? Would man himself willingly descend from the lofty pinnacles of pride? Would he have been ever cured of his haughtiness? Would the illusory clouds of vanity have been dispelled from his head and heart without this divine remedy?

Humility is not the only benefit to be derived from such temptations, afflictions, and interior desolation which leaves the soul weary and disconsolate, depriving it of all emotional sweetness in devotion. For such trials compel us to have recourse to God, to fly from everything displeasing to Him, and to apply ourselves with greater diligence to the practice of virtue. Such afflictions are a kind of Purgatory, which burn away the dross from our souls, and gain us crowns of glory when received with humility and patience.

The soul, convinced of the above truths, may judge whether or not it should be disturbed and grieves at losing a taste for devotional exercises or being engulfed in interior temptations. And it may judge too whether or not it is reasonable to attribute to the devil what comes from God, and to mistake the tokens of His tenderness for marks of His indignation.

On such an occasion all the soul needs do is to humble itself in the sight of God; to persevere and bear with patience the disgust it finds in exercises of devotion; to conform to the divine will, and try to preserve equanimity of soul by humble acquiescence to His decrees. For such is the will of our Father, Who is in heaven.

Instead of languishing in sorrow and dejection, the soul should bloom forth into acts of thanksgiving, establishing itself in peace and submission to the appointments of heaven.

CHAPTER FOURTEEN

The Mode of Behaviour to Be Adopted with Regard to Our Faults

IF IT SHOULD HAPPEN that you commit a fault in word or deed, give way to anger, interrupt your devotions out of some vain curiosity, indulge in immoderate joy or frivolity, entertain suspicious thoughts of your neighbor, or succumb to any failing, be not disquieted. Even if you fail often, succumbing to a fault against which you have made firm resolutions, do not permit such failure to depress and afflict you, considering yourself incapable of amendment, and careless in your devotion. For such troublesome thoughts torture the soul and consume much valuable time.

Neither should you dwell too long in sifting the various circumstances of your faults, such as the thoroughness of deliberation or degree of consent; for such considerations only serve to perplex your mind, both before and after confession, and fill you with uneasiness.

You would not be so much molested with these cares were you well aware of your own inherent weakness, and the conduct you should adopt towards God Almighty after committing such faults. Anxiety and dejection of mind do no good, but only disturb and depress the spirit. By turning to Him, however, with great humility and affection,

227

you are manifesting the proper mode of behavior. And this is to be advocated as regards great faults as well as peccadilloes, not only in those faults occasioned by sloth and tepidity, but even those occasioned by malice itself.

This point is not adequately understood by many; for instead of practicing this great lesson of filial confidence in the goodness and mercy of God, their spirits are so wasted that they are as ineffectual in the execution of a good work as they are in its conception. Thus they lead a miserable, languishing existence, by preferring their own weak imaginations to sound wholesome doctrine in which their welfare consists.

CHAPTER FIFTEEN

The Soul Without Loss of Time Should Compose Itself and Make Steady Progress

As OFTEN AS YOU are guilty of any fault, great or small, frequent or rare, you should adopt the following procedure as soon as you are aware of what you have done. Consider your own weakness, and humbly have recourse to God, saying to Him with a calm and loving confidence: "Thou hast seen, O my God, that I did what I could; Thou hast seen my impotence and, as Thou hast given me the grace to repent, I beseech Thee to add to my pardon the grace never to offend Thee again."

Once you have finished this prayer, do not torture yourself with anxious thoughts on your forgiveness, but without further adverting to your fall, proceed in your devotions with humility and ease, seeking the same tranquillity and peace of mind as before.

This method is to be observed as often as the fault is repeated though it were a thousand times, with as much sincerity and fervor after the last fault as after the first. For this is the way we return immediately to God, Who, like a tender father, is ready to receive us as often as we come to Him. Such a practice also prevents loss of time in fruitless anxiety which only ruffles the serenity of the mind, and prevents it from resuming its usual calmness and fidelity.

I ardently wish that those who grow disconsolate upon committing faults would study well this spiritual secret. They would soon understand how different is their state from a humble cheerful mind where peace and tranquillity reign. They would soon understand the utter fruitlessness and loss of time caused by anxiety and worry.

THOUGHTS ON DEATH

*Every moment of our lives we stand
on the brink of eternity*

Twelve Advantages to Be Derived from the Contemplation of Death

1. Contemplation of death enables us to judge properly and prevents our being imposed upon in all affairs.

With nothing we came into this world, and with nothing shall we leave it. Why then should we consume our very lives in the accumulation of riches?

No one is to accompany us out of this world; why then are we so fond of creatures?

The stench and corruption of the grave in which the pampered body is the prey of the lowest vermin show us the folly of carnal pleasures.

In our narrow cell beneath the earth among the meanest things of creation, when our very blanket of soil may be trampled upon by the meanest beggar, then we shall be freed of the vanity of seeking distinction and preference over others.

2. It is our best instructor through life, laying down but one simple rule, which is the direction of all our acts to one last end.

This consideration drives away all the petty troubles which punctuate this life with unfailing regularity: it steadies us on the course and sustains us on the journey.

3. It teaches us to know ourselves, one of the essential points of true wisdom.

4. It teaches us to despise all that this world can offer, and is the solace of all true servants of God.

5. It is like ice, and helps to chill and deaden the fire of concupiscence; it is a bridle which curbs our sensual appetites.

6. It is a continual source of humiliation, a specific remedy against pride and vanity.

7. It is an excellent preservative against sin. "In all thy works be mindful of thy last end, and thou shalt never sin." Eccl. VII: 40.

8. It brings exasperated minds back to peace and reconciliation. Whoever considers seriously that a certain and unavoidable death will one day bring him before the Judge Who shows no mercy but to those who show mercy to others, he will easily be induced to forgive.

9. It is an antidote against the pleasures and vanities of the world. Thus the prince who once placed a jester in a crazy chair over a large fire told him very justly, seeing the jester's uneasiness, that life should be considered like a defective chair which at any hour, at any moment, might fall to pieces; and the fire beneath the prince represented as the fires of hell which every one should hold in dread.

10. It teaches us a provident economy with regard to our salvation, by setting before our eyes the transitory character of this life, and the necessity of laying up a treasure of good works while it is in our power to do so.

11. It induces us to embrace penances with a cheerful spirit.

12. It encourages us to persevere in the way of penance with unshakable firmness.

THOUGHTS ON PENANCE

Penance is the only pathway to God, once we have been separated from Him in sin. By penance I mean either penance of heart or an active penance. The one is effective, the other affective, and both must be united as the several circumstances of our condition require.

An active or effective penitence is to be utilized when sickness or any voluntary affliction befalls us, or when through a penitential spirit, we discipline ourselves.

In afflictions we practice active penitence in the following situations:

1. As often as we receive crosses with the intention of receiving them as just punishments from a tender parent solicitous for our reform; or as the sentence of a merciful judge who inflicts a penalty in this life in order to spare us in the next.

2. As often as we confess our sins with true repentance, and receive the punishment with due submission.

That these two interior acts may make a deep impression on our hearts they may be accompanied by the following reflections:

a. If the crimes for which we are punished were to be weighed against our sufferings, how light would the atonement be in comparison with our guilt!

b. All that we endure has been decreed in the providence of God.

c. All our sufferings are to our ultimate advantage, as they satisfy for our offences.

d. We suffer too that we may come to a realization of our own wickedness, for we seldom advert to this subject before we feel the hand of God.

e. If by the sacrament of penance we are already in the state of grace, affliction is sent as a means of satisfying the divine justice for the temporal punishment due to our sins.

f. The punishment due to mortal sin is eternal damnation, and irrevocable banishment from the sight of God if one is not repentant.

g. Millions have perished who perhaps were guilty of but one mortal sin after baptism, and many of them were surprised by death the moment it was committed.

In order to apply these truths to our own case when any affliction befalls us, we ought to retire into the depths of our hearts, and reason thus with ourselves:

"Is it not an article of faith that when I first sinned mortally after baptism, I made myself unworthy of all but the reprobates in hell? O my God, if such were actually my fate, how many years should I have already passed in that place of horror! If I consider my first mortal sin, what must I not have suffered in that fiery furnace to this time, and what might I not expect to suffer for all eternity!

"It is through Thy mercy alone, O my God,

that I was not in hell from that first moment I deserved it, that I am not there at this moment, that I may still hope never to go there; and it is through Thy mercy that Thou has not dealt with me as Thou hast with those miserable wretches who now burn there for all eternity.

"Instead of those horrible unending torments, from which You have graciously exempted me, Thou art pleased to send this affliction; and yet I murmur, am impatient and rebellious. What I now suffer cannot possibly last long; what I deserved is eternal!"

An active penitence is exercised by depriving ourselves of any satisfaction of body or mind, with the intention of making some atonement to the divine justice by bearing patiently any contempt or injury, and offering it to the Almighty in expiation of our offenses.

AFFECTIVE PENITENCE OF HEART

This is acquired by grace, and our cooperation —"the grace of God with me." *I Cor. 15, 10.*

The means appointed by providence for obtaining grace is to ask for it—"Ask and you shall receive." Let us pray and strive to obtain it.

HOW WE ARE TO ASK FOR IT

We should ask for affective penitence by forming acts repeatedly throughout the day, by words suitable to the affection God is pleased to instill within our hearts. Let us say: "My God, why did I ever offend Thee; and why, since I have been so miserable, do I not conceive a sorrow for it equal to that of the greatest penitents? How lamentable it is to forfeit my baptismal grace, purchased with Thy Sacred Blood! What ingratitude on my part! What gracious mercy on Thine to pardon such a wretch!

"I now discern, O my God and Father, the excess of Thy love by the incredible patience You have shown me. Thou didst spare me in existence when I brazenly rebelled against Thee."

The words of the devout penitents expressed in the Holy Scriptures will best suit the occasion.

"O God, be merciful to me a sinner."

"Father, I have sinned against heaven and before Thee. I am no longer worthy to be called Thy son."

"Against Thee alone have I sinned, and done evil in Thy sight."

"A contrite and humble heart Thou wilt not despise." *Ps. 50.*

Similar quotations may be utilized.

HOW WE ARE TO LABOR TO ATTAIN IT

Let us consider attentively those motives which are most likely to affect our hearts.

The infinite goodness of God, as evidenced by our very existence.

The greatness of His divine majesty, which has no need of us.

The severity of His just vengeance, which might at once destroy us forever.

It would be wise to consult books on the above subject.

Let us sigh and lament in the presence of God for having offended Him, if these reflections move our hearts; but if we remain cold and indifferent, let us lament our insensibility.

Let us beg of the divine goodness with the Samaritan woman, the water of life. "Lord, give me this water!" One penitential tear can disarm the anger of heaven.

When you ask your celestial Father to give you your daily bread, remember to pray for the bread of tears; that ought to be the daily bread of sinners.

When moved to perform some good action, such as an alms, fasting, or some penitential work or personal deprivation, offer it to God, beseeching Him to bestow on you what you yourself are unable to obtain, i.e., a spirit of penance and sincere contrition for offenses.

Once a week read over these reflections—for example on Saturday or Sunday.

Make it a rule, if you desire to succeed, every day to set apart half an hour to be spent in reading some pious book under these two regulations.

1. Choose such books as will most efficaciously stir up a penitential spirit in your heart.

2. Consider with great attention such passages as seem to affect you in particular, and lead you to an interior and affective spirit of penance.

Assist daily at the Sacrifice of the Mass, the principal object of devotion for the penitent heart, since Jesus Christ is there offered for our sins; and assist also to merit grace for the necessities of life. Join with the priest in offering the sublime sacrifice to God for this dual purpose.

If you have enjoyed this book, consider making your next selection from among the following . . .

Raised from the Dead. Fr. Hebert...................13.50
Autobiography of St. Margaret Mary.................. 4.00
Thoughts and Sayings of St. Margaret Mary........... 3.00
The Voice of the Saints. Comp. by Francis Johnston.... 5.00
The 12 Steps to Holiness and Salvation. St. Alphonsus.. 6.00
The Rosary and the Crisis of Faith. Cirrincione/Nelson.. 1.25
Sin and Its Consequences. Cardinal Manning.......... 5.00
Fourfold Sovereignty of God. Cardinal Manning........ 5.00
Catholic Apologetics Today. Fr. Most................ 8.00
Dialogue of St. Catherine of Siena. Transl. Thorold..... 9.00
Catholic Answer to Jehovah's Witnesses. D'Angelo...... 8.00
Twelve Promises of the Sacred Heart. (100 cards)....... 5.00
St. Aloysius Gonzaga. Fr. Meschler..................10.00
The Love of Mary. D. Roberto...................... 7.00
Begone Satan. Fr. Vogl............................ 2.00
The Prophets and Our Times. Fr. R. G. Culleton.......10.00
St. Therese, The Little Flower. John Beevers.......... 4.50
Mary, The Second Eve. Cardinal Newman............ 2.50
Devotion to Infant Jesus of Prague. Booklet........... .75
The Faith of Our Fathers. Cardinal Gibbons..........13.00
The Wonder of Guadalupe. Francis Johnston........... 6.00
Apologetics. Msgr. Paul Glenn..................... 9.00
Baltimore Catechism No. 1........................ 3.00
Baltimore Catechism No. 2........................ 4.00
Baltimore Catechism No. 3........................ 7.00
An Explanation of the Baltimore Catechism. Kinkead...13.00
Bible History. Schuster............................10.00
Blessed Eucharist. Fr. Mueller.....................13.00
Catholic Catechism. Fr. Faerber.................... 5.00
The Devil. Fr. Delaporte.......................... 5.00
Dogmatic Theology for the Laity. Fr. Premm..........15.00
Evidence of Satan in the Modern World. Cristiani...... 8.50
Fifteen Promises of Mary. (100 cards)............... 5.00
Life of Anne Catherine Emmerich. 2 vols. Schmoger...37.50
Life of the Blessed Virgin Mary. Emmerich...........13.50
Prayer to St. Michael. (100 leaflets)................ 5.00
Prayerbook of Favorite Litanies. Fr. Hebert........... 8.50
Preparation for Death. (Abridged). St. Alphonsus...... 7.00
Purgatory Explained. Schouppe.....................12.50
Purgatory Explained. (pocket, unabr.). Schouppe....... 5.00
Spiritual Conferences. Tauler......................10.00
Trustful Surrender to Divine Providence. Bl. Claude.... 4.00
Wife, Mother and Mystic. Bessieres.................. 7.00
The Agony of Jesus. Padre Pio...................... 1.00

Prices guaranteed through December 31, 1991.